The Universe Has A Number

The Numerology Guide For Beginners And Discovering Numbers That Resonate With Your Future, Money, Career, Love, And Destiny

Donald B. Grey

Bluesource And Friends

This book is brought to you by Bluesource And Friends, a happy book publishing company.

Our motto is **"Happiness Within Pages"**

We promise to deliver amazing value to readers with our books.

We also appreciate honest book reviews from our readers.

Connect with us on our Facebook page www.facebook.com/bluesourceandfriends and stay tuned to our latest book promotions and free giveaways.

Don't forget to claim your FREE books!

Brain Teasers:

https://tinyurl.com/karenbrainteasers

Harry Potter Trivia:

https://tinyurl.com/wizardworldtrivia

Sherlock Puzzle Book (Volume 2)

https://tinyurl.com/Sherlockpuzzlebook2

Also check out our best seller book

"67 Lateral Thinking Puzzles"

https://tinyurl.com/thinkingandriddles

The Universe Has A Number

The Universe Has A Number

Description

Are you looking for answers and haven't found any of them in the usual places? Do you seek answers to why or how certain things always happen in the same way every time but don't know how to explain it? Are there times when you have a number repeat itself and you look at it constantly trying to figure out why it is always in your life? All along this book, you will find the secret wisdom of how we are all aligned with the numerical code of the whole Universe and how to understand how it influences your life each day.

Numerology is no new thing. Ancient societies and cultures have been studying the life of numbers and how they have a say in the energy of all things since man was erecting structures and learning from their environment. And when have all of these ideas come in handy in modern life? Look around you. How tall is the tallest skyscraper and how was it constructed?

The Universe Has A Number

Numbers. How long have you looked at the same bank account number and maintained a certain level of income in it, wishing for more, and what influences that energy? Numbers. How are you going to get yourself the job you truly want to have with the income you know you deserve? Numbers.

Learning the languages of numbers and the reality behind numerology opens an entire world of wisdom to you, the reader, so that you can uncover an even deeper layer of truth to the life you are already living. Look inside your house and see all the ways numerology may have already influenced your life. Ask yourself what your numbers are and find right away that there is a secret number hidden within you.

Every part of life, from nature to civilization, culture to cosmos, has a number and you are here to know how to discover the true meaning of numerology. Having a handle on how to interpret the number signs that come for you on a life level can show you your true calling, your financial capabilities, your health and wealth, and so much more. Even the name you are given at birth has a number, as well as the date, time, and place of where you were born, giving your whole life a numerical code, a blueprint to success, and all you have to do is 'know your number.'

In this book you will find:

- The ancient history and philosophy of numerology and why it had an impact on culture and society
- How numbers have an effect on nature and govern the cycles of life across the whole planet, as well as the whole cosmos
- Access to your birth number and personality number to help show you the energy of your self

The Universe Has A Number

- How to predict the future with numerology tactics
- The specific meaning behind each number from zero to nine

- Number combinations that have a bigger meaning and purpose
- Messages for you from the Universe as seen through numbers
- How to find love with numerology; dating advice from numbers
- The link between numbers and names
- Numerology in the home, work, and family
- And so much more…

Introduction

Since the beginning of time, we as a human species have dedicated ourselves to the quest for knowledge about how the Universe works. All of the answers to our questions lie in one simple truth: numbers. Ancient societies and cultures have known that a whole world of secret knowledge existed behind the energy of numbers and how they communicate through their language of clear and concise achievement of prediction, managing life cycles, growth of entire civilizations, religious enterprises, questions about life, and so much more.

It's no secret that the language of numbers has something to say and has always had its place in our lives. Even a matter as simple as balancing your checking account or getting a job with the right amount of income has a link to the energy and power of what those numbers mean to your whole life.

The Universe Has A Number

As you read this book, you will learn how the history of numerology has built and torn down many buildings, religious beliefs, and whole communities founded on the science of numbers. You will learn how to determine which numbers have more meaning to you specifically based on your birthday, name, and other matters. You will get acquainted with your own understanding of how to interpret numbers to align your life in positive ways, and treat each number as a symbol or input of what kind of wisdom you should use in certain life circumstances.

Your life has a number and so does your love, health, career, name, and even your car and the building that you live in. All of our determination to have the answers about how to get where we want to go lies in the magic Universe of Numerology, and all you have to do to get there is ask each number what it has to offer you.

The Universe Has A Number

We all have an understanding of numbers and what they mean from a mathematical standpoint, but what about the literal message they convey through the energy of all life and all matter. The Universe does indeed have a number. What's yours?

Chapter 1: History of Numerology

We are people of knowledge and we have always wanted to find the key to the world and the Universe. Many of us have looked for the answers at a place in time that could only show a certain fraction of knowledge to us. All of us have believed numerous things about why the world works a certain way or doesn't, and the key to a lot of these answers lies in the magic of numbers. 2,000 BCE saw a rise at the beginning of seeking wisdom from the world of numbers, and the term numerology was never used to understand these teachings and this wisdom.

A certain member of a culture of knowledge seekers, called Pythagoras, appeared hundreds of years later to begin to outline and describe the hidden messages and meanings in numbers, and related them to a

The Universe Has A Number

variety of life wisdoms including how we make money, where we find out partners, what it looks like in regard to music, and cultural concepts of truth that were related to how individuals paired with groups to create workers, religious sects, priesthoods, and a score of other human groupings.

All of the theories of Pythagoras were considered to be a lot like what we call mathematics in our world, and he had a lot more to do with the messages of numbers, not their arithmetic qualities. Although he described numbers as a way to alter ideas through equations and build worlds through calculation, he was also expressing the concept as numbers having strength or energetic power that aligned certain things in the world with each other.

The power of synchronicity was eluded to in his teachings, but all of his written texts were lost or destroyed, but also perhaps not yet discovered. The teachings of Pythagoras were carried down by his

The Universe Has A Number

students and passed over to the world of common math, losing all of the musical attributes, all of the magic, and most of the meaning. All of his students began to move away from his position on numbers as his practices and knowledge fell out of fashion and favor with the more practical realities of the time.

All over the world, however, other cultures were expressing an interest in the power of numbers. It was never secluded and discovered by one person or group. The energy of numbers was brought into the religious cults, ancient texts and rituals, structures of temples, sacred buildings, and all of the places where people worshipped the Gods and Goddesses.

Tons of ideas circulated about how each number had a meaning, a purpose, a sacred identity and much of what was taught or discovered had an element of truth to it, allowing for a large, human evolution in the discovery of numerology. Practices of numerology have evolved over the centuries, and in today's modern world, the magic of numbers has a lot of sway in certain groups, communities, and all over the internet of information.

Many people today are turning toward numerology to find answers to many of their questions regarding their love relationships, career paths, health and wealth, topics of destiny, how to achieve your true-life purpose, and where to ask for the right money win, such as in the lottery or through gambling.

Other circles seek the magic of numbers to interpret the more esoteric aspects of life. There is a strong link to numerology and the tarot, but also astrology and other sciences of understanding the soul. So, many of us continue to attempt to decipher the correct meaning behind all of these ideas and one hundred thousand or more books have been written on the topic of numerology.

The Universe Has A Number

This book is going to reveal more than you have seen before on the internet or in the world of books. The logic of it is simpler than you may even realize yet, and the people throughout history who have searched for this secret knowledge have only scratched the surface of what is really true of the numbers of the universe.

How do we truly know the actual purpose of each number and why it exists? What does each number tell you about yourself, your past, your present, your future? How will each number guide you forward in your life, like it has for so many ancient cultures and civilizations?

The answers are here in this book and the history ask you to open your mind about what you may not know about numerology. All of the histories show a number has a life force and will show you a story of light and energy. Every person, group, or culture who practiced the knowledge of numbers knew that each individual number was more than just a number, and was more of the energy of life and a presence to behold.

We are not without our numbers and having a knowledge of what they mean, how they truly answer our life questions, and what to do with them in the presence of life moments, is what our ancestors brought to us through the ages and here into these pages.

While you read this book, think of all the people who came before you who already had this knowledge and have already discovered its power. It has a name for a reason, and the name is numerology.

Chapter 2: Numerology and Nature

Numbers are everywhere, not just in written form as a 6 or a 9. Where you look at numbers and see them in their written form as they appear to all of the eyes shows us how they are shaped and how they can each be identified. All that really shows is a signature of the energy of that number. Most people look at the following sequence of numbers 65845289911214 and only see digits. The Universe looks at the sequence of numbers and has a whole world of information open up to it. It is the language of numerals that shows us how they can be written and expressed, but it is the vibration of numbers that appears in the nature of all things.

Plenty of places all over the Earth elicit numerical energy. You have to look very hard to notice it, but it is there. All sunshine coming through the trees and

The Universe Has A Number

dappling the forest floor and leaves has a number frequency. All children running through a garden hose in the hot summer heat, splashing drops off the water in every direction, have a number sequence. All washing lines with clothes hanging off of them, blowing in the wind, have a number sequence. And even the food you eat from your plate has a number sequence.

Numbers are everywhere and are in everything. As we look around our lives, we may hardly notice these ideas or realities because we have not known to look at them. They are a part of how we make choices, and we don't even realize how these vibrations of numerical energy are impacting our daily outputs and incomes.

One of the most wonderful ways to observe numerical energy is in the frequency of life on Earth. The world of nature demonstrated a whole other scope of understanding in the life of numbers, and all of the world has a powerful life force energy that

The Universe Has A Number

creates a unique energetic number sequence that can be seen all over the place: The Fibonacci Sequence.

The Fibonacci Sequence was a numerical discovery founded by a man studying math in the early 1000s and who never fully understood in his lifetime the power of his discovery. The number sequence is a lovely pattern of numbers that appeared organically in a wide variety of elements on Earth. From seashells to honeycomb, from whirlpools to sunflower faces. All of these have an acquaintance through their numerical life force energy, discovered and demonstrated by the person known as Fibonacci.

All of these numbers form an energetic spiral of information, also known as the golden ratio, and the energy of a spiral of energy is the strongest in the whole universe. It has a quality of energy that links to the wisdom of all life and all beings in the Universe, and is demonstrated in several places throughout nature, even in the human body.

The Universe Has A Number

Mathematical moments are recorded through science and physics in an attempt to arrive at an understanding of how such numerical power and life force could exist in so many places in our world. Here is the answer to that query and you will only see it in this book: The Fibonacci Sequence, or the golden ratio, is the most elegant numerical code for understanding the life force energy in all living things. It has been broken down and studied everywhere in the world and never truly understood, because most researchers and mathematicians can only see digits or geometrical shapes and not energy. Energy is the key to understanding numerology and the numerology in nature is all energy.

The power of numbers lies in how you can comprehend the energy behind each one. In the example of the Fibonacci Sequence, you can see the elegance of the numbers aligning with each other and expanding as a swirl of information that leads outward from a primal center. Patterns in nature are all working toward becoming like this energetic

The Universe Has A Number

frequency, and it is part of the evolution of all things to look forward to becoming as exquisite as this sequence of numbers.

The number pattern is 1, 1, 2, 3, 5, 13, 21, 34, 55. The elegance of the numbers shows a system of enlargement that follows an equation unlike all others and has its essential energy in strength and life force. It has power and shows how all living things begin at a small central point, and expand and enlarge over time.

Numerologists study this sequence in order to find the link between it and other energies in the world, not just in nature, to recreate this same numerical power and force. It has been used to erect tall buildings and also has been used in varies kinds of surgical procedures and healing practices. It has been used to solve problems in the world of architecture and design, and is equally as valuable in the reality of strategic money-making processes.

The Universe Has A Number

This number sequence speaks volumes when it comes to the science and history of numerology. Asking all of the numbers in the world how they make their energetic form is the language behind understanding numerology and how it works. All of the signs and symbols that you see have numerical energy. When you see a number repeat itself in any walk of life, you are being shown a message of energy and have to discover the purpose of that number, and why it is aligning with you at any given moment.

Ask yourself what numbers have popped up regularly for you and decide how well you know that numerical energy. The number itself is always more than just a digit; it is a key to unlock a doorway to a whole other world of understanding your own power and the power of the whole Universe.

Chapter 3: Positive and Negative Energies of Numbers

While we are looking out our energies and our frequencies of numbers, let's talk a little bit about what that means in the first place. All things in life carry an energy vibration or frequency. There are a number of ways this can be expressed in the world and through our lives, and for the most part, it is all invisible to the naked eye.

The energy of everything has a way of suggesting, or showing, to us what our own energy frequency might be as a result of other vibrational qualities in our life cycles. You may be wondering right now how well you are looking when you see yourself in the mirror or in a photograph taken of you and, that "feeling" has an energy to it. The places you go to get your groceries have energy. All of the food you buy and put in your shopping cart has energy. Your shopping cart has energy. Even the money that you take out of your wallet to pay for the groceries has energy to it.

Looking at all of the things in your life and beginning to see the value as all of our life's energy, you may begin to experience a new belief in how you have been looking at all parts of your life and the energies within them. We are either high in energetic vibration or we are low. That can be called either positive or negative. The lower your vibration, the more negative you may feel, or the more negative your shopping bag filled with frozen pizza might be.

After you start to engage with and understand the knowledge of how our whole world is an energy field, then you can start to adapt to understanding the knowledge of numerical energy. Wisdom seekers have often described numerology as the energy of numbers and the life force of arithmetic, but when all is said and done, the most important thing to note is that every music note has a vibration equivalent to the energetic vibration of a number.

The Universe Has A Number

Imagine plucking the low C string on a cello. As you pluck the string, it vibrates and emits a sound that correlates to an energetic vibration assigned to the letter C on the solfeggio scale. The scale itself is all a numerical organization of light waves of energetic vibrations. All chords are a series of numbers, vibrating into sound waves. All sounds made in all of the universe are really just numbers shaking with the vibration of a wave of energy.

Digging further into the quality of energy and how it impacts numbers, all numbers are naturally positive in their energy and do not have negative vibrations. However, some negative scenarios in life elude to certain numbers or strings of numbers that can be identified as negative, because of the circumstances they are linked to. Most people look at the number 666 and see a signal of evil or of the Devil; however, this number has a truly positive light. The number 6 itself has a very strong vibration of love and friendship, as well as community and circles of power and industry. The family and home life has a powerful

6 intonation as well as work-related success and career climbing.

The real truth about positive and negative numbers is that there are no inherently negative numbers, only inherently negative situations. You may have a good feeling about a number because of how it always manages to show up in a lucky moment and keeps you feeling light as free, while another number happens to show up at times of turmoil, low-energy, vibration, and so you associate a negative feeling or energy with this number.

The best way to describe negative energies in regard to numbers is that a number arrives in you when you need it the most, and having a negative feeling about a number means that you are being shown how the number has a message of positive life force for you to work with and understand. The number has a way of guiding you and allowing you to notice what may be in need of some attention in your life.

The Universe Has A Number

Try this exercise: he next time you see a number pop up that you are regularly seeing as a bad number in your life, open this book to Chapter 5 and look at the meaning of the number you are seeing. Ask yourself what the number is trying to teach you and how all of your energy is asking you to give thought to the energy of what that number is offering to you as energy. It could be the very thing that shows you how well you look in that picture or how hungry you are for fresh vegetables instead of frozen pizza.

Learning how to understand numerology means looking for the hidden meaning in the energy of the numbers themselves and what kinds of messages they may carry for you. All numbers have a positive vibration and all negative situations have numerical solutions.

Chapter 4: Numerology and Astrology

Numbers always connect to the rhythm and life cycles of the planet, and the world of the cosmos. A great deal of our lives have been spent studying these remarkable orbs and how they influence the world we live in and our own identities. The structure of self-knowledge, known as astrology, demonstrates the mystical quality of how our position on the Earth, the time we are born, the date we are born, and the position of the planets and the stars in the sky have an impact on our personality and how we choose to lead our lives.

Astrology has grown in popularity over the ages and has a significant amount of its origins in the world of numbers. After all, understanding the planets in the sky and how their position affects our lives has a great deal to do with math and science, and the reality of

The Universe Has A Number

numbers aligning in a perfect way to make you who you are.

The exact moment you are born, you will be living on the Earth as a being of energy on your own. Before you are born, you are in the energy of your mother's life and not entirely by yourself. The place of your birth shows you exactly where to pinpoint the level of knowledge from the planets and how you will be considered on the astrological chart.

There are 12 astrological signs and they follow the seasons of the year as much as they follow the rotation of the Earth around the sun, and numbers are behind every inch of it all. The twelve signs are as follows: Aries (March 21-April 19), Taurus (April 20–May 20), Gemini (May 21- June 20), Cancer (June 21-July 22), Leo (July 23-August 22), Virgo (August 23-September 22), Libra (September 23- October 22), Scorpio (October 23- November 21), Sagittarius (November 22- December 21), Capricorn (December

The Universe Has A Number

22-January 19), Aquarius (January 20- February 18), and Pisces (February 19- March 20).

All of these astrological symbols are depicted by a certain figure or creature in order to associate it with the astronomy of the stars. The Ram is the Aries sign, while the Taurus is the cosmic bull. The Gemini sign is represented as the solar twins as the Cancer is symbolized by the crab constellation. The Sign of Leo is an obvious Lion, while the Virgin is a Virgo. Libra is the scales, the only inanimate object in the zodiac, representing the cause of justice in the cosmos as the Scorpio has the piercing, stinging tail of the Scorpion constellation. The Sagittarius is the centaur in the sky, while the Capricorn is the climbing mountain goat. Aquarius is shown as the Water Bearer, pouring his cup into the heavens, while the Pisces is a double swirling fish, head to tail in a circle of life.

Each of these symbols has a numerical map in the stars, just as they each have a number association with the month of the year, and the span of time between

The Universe Has A Number

each symbol. Portions of astrology allow for even deeper knowledge and understanding of how your astrological symbol has numerical meaning, and all of that has to do with how you calculate your birthdate to understand your birth number, which you will discover in Chapter 6.

We all have the urge to discover our true personality and having an astrological symbol to guide you is only the beginning. The purpose of astrology is to give you a basic ground point to leap off from so that you can further explore and examine the deeper meaning behind so much of your true self, and your purpose in the energy of all that is around you, including numbers.

After you learn more about how your energy works with the energy of all things around you, you can begin to truly realize and understand the capacity of the cosmic forces of nature, to have a force on your energy in determining the energy of your whole life and your experiences. Astrology is only half of it.

The Universe Has A Number

Having a good grasp of your Sun sign and your Moon sign is a great beginning to learning more about your identity, but once you start to add numerology to the picture, you give yourself a more accurate perception of who you are in the reality of your life.

When you are asking yourself on a daily basis how your astrological sign is impacting your choices or your experience, you may add a few queries through the numbers of the day into the mix. For example, if your birth number is 9 and you are living on the day of April 15, 2019, you would figure the date down to one small number and make a decision about how that number compares or relates to your birth number, or what you may want to align with energetically for the day. The month of April is the fourth month, and therefore resonates with the energy of the number 4. The year 2019 will be added together to create a smaller, whole number (see below).

April 15, 2019 can break down like this:

The Universe Has A Number

$4 + 15 + 2019 = 4 + 1 + 5 + 2 = 12 = 1 + 2 = 3$

The number 3 is the daily number. Looking at your birthday number, 9, you can already see a relationship between the two:

$3 + 3 + 3 = 9$

9 divided by $3 = 3$

The numbers have quality energy together because they bond well and have unification in their order of alignment. Once you have an idea of how each number might relate to each other, you can start to identify how the number of the day might impact your own energetic frequency. For example, for you as a 9, the number 3 means you will have a lot of energetic harmonies, and will have a lot of positive energy surrounding your creativity and your passionate side of life. You may find it easier to paint or draw, or you may find it beneficial to take a tango dancing class on a 3 day, instead of a 2 or a 4. See the reality of number energy?

Astrology is how you find your number and the meaning behind your symbol. All the symbols in the zodiac have a number associated with them from 1-12, Aries being the first and Pisces being the 12th. As you begin to study your own personal numerology, you can start to see how your zodiac symbols can paint a picture of your personality and your identity, and how that energetic numerical frequency can be affected by all of the energy of the Universe. Carefully studying your number position in reality based on your astrology can assist and guide you into a better understanding of how to live harmoniously in your life, relationships, career, and adventurous life.

Chapter 5: From Zero to Nine: All the Numbers You Need to Know

Numbers all have a meaning and a vibration, while each one has its own unique shape and description as well. Every number wants to describe a lesson to you as it moves through the Universe of space, time, weight, and structure. All of the elements on the Periodic Table are associated with a specific number and another number based on their weight. All elements are classified numerically as are all other unseen lessons in the Universe of information.

Most ideas about numbers on Earth and in human minds are related to the institution of mathematics and all of its elegant branches of thought. Without the basic language of math, we wouldn't be able to truly comprehend the language of numbers and how they can appear in the world of knowledge, but also the sensations around us; this is what math cannot explain to you.

Math has a way of telling you how numbers will allow certain things to occur, but it will never tell you why. That is why numerology exists: it is the why behind the language of numbers and has a way of informing you on a completely different level about the world all around you.

As you begin to look through these pages, you will find out more and more about how numbers can impact your life in a variety of ways, and what to do when they show up in your life at certain times. How you look at each number is of great importance so that you can learn the personality trait of each one, and how to identify what they are wanting to communicate with you at certain times in your life.

We will discuss every number, from 0-9, in this chapter to give you a better understanding of how each one has a unique vibration and personality

The Universe Has A Number

assigned to it, so that you will have a better understanding of how each one is trying to communicate information to you.

As you read through each of these number portfolios, get to know each one of these digits in a new way, as you have possibly never seen them before. Let them speak for themselves and ask each one how it has come into your life before, in a special or curious way that you may not have noticed in the past.

Zer0

The number zero is the entrance hall to knowing a number. The round shape of the zero is a door that leads to a whole land of welcoming information about how numbers are and what they want to show us. The number itself has no official value assigned to it and is, therefore, a neutral vibration in the realm of energy. It has a way of allowing for all numbers to be increased in a certain way as well. Consider the numbers 10, 20, 30, 40, 50, and so on. Each one of these numbers would only be a measly 1, 2, 3, 4, 5, etc. without the vibration and power of the zero. Allowing your ideas about how numbers are energy to inform you here, let's look even deeper into the possibilities of a number like zero. As you can see in its shape, it is an oval and has a way of expanding other digits into a larger number, without altering the vibration of the other number's frequencies. The lesson from this is that all numbers attached to the digit zero will be empowered energetically by the accompaniment of the zero and will have a higher frequency than they had before. Take a look at this number: 1,000,000,000. That is a huge number, isn't it? One billion, to be exact, and if you didn't have all of those zeros attached to the end of the 1, then it wouldn't amount to very much at all. How you view numbers now may have changed a little bit, because you are now seeing it as a power or energy and not just a digit.

The zero awakens the essence of the energy of each number and widens it into an even bigger capability, as it has the capacity to powerfully open the world of

The Universe Has A Number

information through its circular opening. All you need to do is add a zero to any number and you will have an increase in the energy and vibration of that number.

Not all numbers work well with a zero in front of them. For example, if you see the number 0.00000000000000000001, you may look at it and see the opposite impact. And this is also the unique power of zero that no other number has. Just as well as it can empower a number with its energy, it can also diminish a number with its energy, and this is how it maintains neutral energy. It has the power to do both equally and will never change in that language of energetic ability and power.

As you embrace your new understanding of the number zero, look for it all around you in your life; on your receipts, in your bank account, in your refrigerator or with all of your food, at the mall, or on your phone. It is everywhere you look each day and has a way to bring more or less to every numerical vibration.

ONE

The number 1 comes after zero in accordance with the numerical order of energy and vibration, and has the energy of new beginning and the power and life force of initiation. It is a groundbreaking moment in a lot of ways and begins a new cycle of counting from the top or starting point. Most of the time, when counting, you start with 1 and not zero, and there is a good reason for this. The number one has its frequency and energy as a lesson in oneness, not only as single digit energy. To understand this concept, you have to realize that any 1 can have a singular appearance and that it can vibrate the energy of simplicity and have an alignment with purity, wholeness, and light in its singular way, and will always bare strength in its simplicity and limitlessness.

But the 1 is also a number of all. It tells the story of everything and everyone as one whole energy and has its power in unification and purpose of life with all things and all matters. The number 1 is life flowing into itself, regenerating and renewing all over again, each and every day. You will only know how to write a number 1 from the top to the bottom or from the bottom to the top. It is a straight line of wisdom and it holds a lot of powerful energy in order to demonstrate the singularity and uniqueness of all things, but also the unity and oneness of all things as well.

All of the number 1s around you have a message of renewal, rebirth, growth, possibility, beginning, wholeness, uniqueness, oneness, identity, purpose, and power in the "I" of all things as well as power in the "Oneness" of all things. A little 1 goes a long way in the identity of our Universe and has the power to let you know a singular detail, or the power of everything in the cosmos and it hasn't changed at all since day 1.

TWO

The Universe Has A Number

This number brings together a new vibration from the impact of adding two 1s to each other. The entire world assigns new energy to itself as it increases in value through the mathematical application of addition. It is a simple matter to add two 1s to get a 2, and all you have to do is energetically bind them together to transform the straight line into a new shape that curves at the top and lands on the ground with a horizontal foot to balance its top out.

This elegant formation has been known to elicit a response of energy that has an appearance in nature. One of the most graceful creatures on Earth is the swan and has a neck shape in accordance with its body that resembles the shape of the number 2. Swans are animals that mate for life and have a strong symbolism in the energy of love and the vibration of togetherness.

When you look at number 2, it has a way of offering you an immediate idea or feeling about how it is in the energy of its being. Two is always better than one,

The Universe Has A Number

they say, and the energy and vibration of number 2 are about partnership and love. The number itself does not "feel" this way; it vibrates this information into the Universe of all life and all matter, and so when you see the number two, you can understand its hidden message to you.

Twos are all about you and me, togetherness, a couple of people, love bonds, marriage, partnership, comradery, pair bonding in the elements and atoms of the Universe, and compatibility. The two will always be a couple and nothing can ever separate a two into energy after it has been bonded. Not even math, division and subtraction, can manipulate the power and life force of the number 2.

THREE

The third digit in the walk up of numbers after you welcome the neutrality of zero is 3. The number three welcomes powerful triangular energy that unites all three sides of something to bring about a more bonded energy and life force. The Holy Trinity was a major aspect of religious understanding and had the power of three as well as the energetic vibration of equality and passive trust. All 3s in the Universe behave in accordance with the energy of life cycles and the wisdom of first, middle, and last; or beginning, middle, and end. The energy format in the 3 is depicted in the rounded shape that stands like an E and faces to the right. The three is open and available to all of the energy of the Universe and has its greatest power and strength in all works of art and creation.

Three is a number of creativity and has the power to align all creative forces in order to demonstrate the energy of making and becoming. When you hear about a major artist developing their great work of art in oil on the canvass to be revealed at an art opening, they are working in accordance with the vibration of the number 3. All the energies involved in this number bring about the divine forces of creation to allow for more of what the Universe wants to bring to it, through the hands of people, through the birth of new life, through the ebb and flow of all life cycles, and through the building of structures that improve the energy of all things.

The number 3 brings with it the vibration of living a creative life, welcoming all good things as they transform from beginning to middle to end, and then start again; the power of 3 brings into your life an openness to the power of thoughtful crafting, making, doing, structuring, labor of artistic forms and all that that implies. 3 is always a creative number and has a way of informing you about how to welcome the life force of art and structure, and the value of openness in its energy.

FOUR

The number 4 is where you begin to understand how a number can force you into an energetic balance and dynamic strength, and openness to the primal energy if a number. The number 4 has a strength in all its sides. Envision a square. A square has four equal sides and has a look of utter power because of how strong it seems in its energetic make-up and life force. The stability of a square and its four angles has a way of telling you that you are never going to have to worry about a thing. A 4 is demanding that you stay put and use your force to become grounded and gain your footing.

All of the 4 energy in the Universe can be found in all of the places that have a groundedness and the quality of stability. Look at a mountain or a rock wall. See a large stone or even a tree with its roots extending out underneath the soil across a forest floor. Here is the 4. Building on its own work as a vibration of power, the four elaborates on the energy of the 2 and the 3 by showing how the unity and partnership of energy used in a creative and artful way, creates the abundant life force and strength of the number 4.

All of your experiences in your life have some connection to a 4 and here is how: your home is a 4, not just in structure, but in the way that you organize it and improve upon it. Your car has a 4 vibration

The Universe Has A Number

because of how it is constructed and how it keeps
your body away from danger while traveling at great
speed on the highway. Your work has a vibration of
the number 4 and all of your career aspirations have a
4 in them, especially when you are in a successful
period of achievement and accolades.

The number 4 is power, force, and strength. It has
brought together all of the sides of a 1 and enveloped
the power of the 2 and the 3 to provide an energy of
stability and groundedness. It is a great relief to have a
4 in your power due to its ability to calm and relax
you. When 4 is around, you don't have to worry;
everything is sturdy, safe, and well banded together.
Consider how 4 comes into your life and discover
how well you have stabilized yourself, your work,
your relationships, and or your home.

FIVE

The number 5 also has stability; however, it asks a
little bit more of the mind and not as much of the
physical reality of the number 4. The number 5 works

well on its own and has a way of leading a life of assessment, through listening to the energy of all other things and then transforming that information into a more workable knowledge. The 5 is like the computer that wants to decipher all of the wondrous aspects of all energies and change them into a pattern of relevance and understanding.

The number 5 has a similar shape to that of a 2, but the curved line of it is at the bottom and the straight, horizontal line is at the top. All the five asks is for you to interpret or comprehend what is around you. It is a number that is also very compatible with the assessment of money and finances. A 5 will help you realize all of the energy that you need in your assets as far as dollars are concerned, and have the gift of allowing for a clearer understanding about the energies of dollars and cents.

This is also a number whose energetic purpose and the vibration is all about the learning of information and not just the comprehension. It is the number of education and the formality of looking at the world through the lens of the intellect. A very powerful number indeed, as it no longer needs or requires the dynamic and primal life force energy associated with the numbers 1-4, and has a way of determining and interpreting all of the other energies around it without any effort.

A 5 is all you need to assess, predict, ascertain, learn, compute, understand, process, educate, and decipher. It is a tool of knowledge and has all of its power in learning and understanding. 5 will show you how and why.

SIX

Away from the 5, we walk to the 6, an entirely different energy expression from the last number you made the acquaintance of. The number 6 is a beautiful energy that only wants a connection to all of the other energies around it. Like the 2, the 6 wants us to understand the feelings of emotional matters, the bonds of love, the compassion of friendship, and the energy of togetherness. It happens to be a very powerful love number, although it has a had a very strong and unfortunate affiliation with demonic influences or forces. The power of this number has never had any worrisome or dark energy associated with it, and has had a bad rap ever since it became associated with the Devil.

The number 6 is actually meant to communicate a wandering away from dark energy or life force. It has a way of asking you to let go of your worries, your fears, your doubts, and insecurities, and asks you to embrace a more loving, hopeful, faithful feeling or energy. As much as people want to believe it has dark energy connected to it, the presence of the number 6 is actually a way for you to acknowledge the dark forces in your life so that you can move ahead in a more harmonious manner.

The 6 is a powerful number of harmony and love, friendship, and assessment of what is hurting you in your life that might need to change. A lot of people

The Universe Has A Number

fight with their own inner voices and feelings or inner conflict, resulting in a lot of unfortunate habits and addictions. The 6 is a messenger of awakening to what isn't helping you in your life, or how what is happening in your energy may not be the best for you, and that you will need to shift your focus into a better energetic vibration. An example of this would be asking someone to help you learn about mental health therapies so that you can find a place to heal and grow, instead of living in cycles or thought patterns of sorrow or anger.

The 6 is all about healing and helping. It wants you to awaken to the right path for you and to help you avoid the traumatic moments that can easily be shifted into another part of the alignment with yourself. The number 6 also provides you with the mission of success in your partnerships in friendship and camaraderie with all people in general as you pass through your life. It has the quality of giving you the message of letting yourself find friendship in all places as you grow on your path.

The Universe Has A Number

SEVEN

The number 7 is a beautiful energy that adopts the posture of awakening to a higher aspect of yourself. The number itself is an abundant number and has a lot of purpose for those who are educating themselves in the matters of spiritual awakening and soul alignment. Not all sevens bear this fruit or all sevens have an association with the part of life connected to financial luck. Luck is a sign from a 7 and when you see one in your life a lot, you are likely walking toward a lucky moment, experience, or windfall that you need to pay attention to, and the number 7 is asking you to keep your eyes open for the right moment of luck and abundance.

As the 7 appears to you, notice its shape and form. It has a top line that is horizontal and a swoop or straight line coming from its right-hand top line, down toward the Earth. The 7 is an anchor of awareness to shout out to you, "Hey! Keep your eyes open right in this area of your life! Something is coming up!" It is a message to you to look at all places in your life where 7 wants to ask you for your awareness, so you can see the excitement of abundance and prosperity.

As you ask more of what the 7 can offer, allow it to express its alignment with your future goals and career ideas. It can have a lot to tell you about whether you are on the right path or not. Allow 7 to answer all of your questions about how to act on a lotto ticket or a card game if you are a gambler. The 7 is a voice of powerful wisdom when it comes to accepting the odds and allowing them to work in your favor.

EIGHT

The 8 is so great and we can all see why. It is the only digit that fully closes itself into one continuous and infinite line of energy and has a strong association with the energy of infinity. The 8 is a complete curve into itself and never fully allows for anything to disrupt its flow. It is in accordance with the highest vibrations of energy within the Universe, and is often attributed to the endlessness of all things and the patterns of death and rebirth as a cycle of life in all nature and all matter. The presence of an 8 in your life is incredibly valuable and important, as it arrives at a time when you need all of the power in your life to encircle your acceptance of truth and inevitability. There are times and places for all things, and sometimes we care too much about how we want things to go, instead of the way they will naturally flow in accordance with the laws of energy and plans of life. Creating an act of faith out of the energy of 8 is a great way to respond to its vibration and energy.

There are only two ways the 8 will come to you in your life and they are as follows:

1. An 8 will teach you about how to ask for what you want around issues of financial success and abundance.

2. An 8 will prepare you for the ascension of your inner being by telling you in a friendly way that you have to let go, trust the inevitable, and not try to control everything in your life.

Many people struggle with wanting to create a path, instead of just living the one they are assigned to in their own way as a person who comes to life with a specific purpose. As all of us have seen, allowing ourselves to truly live as our most purposeful selves can be a great challenge, and an 8 will provide you with more understanding of how to flow energetically toward what you actually want and not what you *think* you want.

An 8 will always have powerful advice for how to work with the energy of all life around you instead of swimming against the current. It asks you to go with the flow and trust the inevitable cycles of life as they come and unfold in front of you on your path.

NINE

The Universe Has A Number

The number 9 is the final digit to get to know and it has a lot to say. The 9 is a delicate, curving energy with a powerful impact. How it is shaped shows its distinct similarity to the number 8 just before it, but bears an opening at the bottom. There is a top circle with a tail coming from out of the right side, dropping down to touch the ground. The top part of the nine is a circle of understanding the truth of what the 8 has shown you in your current life experience, while the tail of the nine exposes your acceptance of the truth, opening to whatever cycles of life have pushed you forward on your path to self-discovery, fame, wealth, abundance, and personal pride and joy.

All nines have the energy of awareness as a lesson in enlightenment in accordance with your life purpose or path. Your journey has its own unique qualities; however, we all are seeking to know who we truly are and how to get what we truly want. 9 resembles the answers to the questions you seek and has an authority of quality energy of peace, calm, rest, and admiration for all things in life. It asks you to be present with all of the things you have learned and grown from, and wants you to believe in the power of your own intuition, as you prove your own worth on your journey of life.

Putting the 9 into perspective with all of the numbers before it, 9 is the culmination of all of these energies put together and asks for admittance of truth in all of the numerical vibrations from 1-8. They do not add up to the number 9, but numerology is not math: it is the science of energy through the language of numbers and is therefore not about addition or subtraction at all.

9 will always comfort you as a way of showing you that you have become fully empowered in a certain area in your life, and that you will always have all of the energy you need to fulfill your destiny, goals, and dreams as you advance along your path.

Every Number Wants Another Number

All of these numbers have significant attributes on their own and have a lot of energy in their vibration

The Universe Has A Number

already. So, how do you interpret these numbers
when they are coupled, or tripled, or in a long chain
of various combinations of all of these numbers?

The answer is simple: all of these numbers ask for
each other to come together to form messages of
truth for all energy in the Universe, so as you are
looking at numbers, they are looking at you and
helping you see an important detail that you may not
have noticed before.

Allowing yourself to become more aware of all
numbers in your life can actually provide you with an
important method of deciphering all of the energy
around you. It's not magic; it's energy and vibration,
and since everything is energy, it makes sense that you
would learn to understand and interpret that language.

Every number wants another number because they
have to be available to all circumstances of thought,
experience, ebbs and flows, endings and beginnings,
highs and lows, and all corners of nature, matter, and
life force. When a number comes together with

The Universe Has A Number

another number, or two, or four, and so on, the numbers are communicating at a level of knowledge to share a specific message to you. They are saying, "Look at this sequence and consider this moment. What can you tell yourself about what is happening right now, and are you paying attention to all that is happening around you?"

Many numbers are very popular among esoteric communities and psychics for possessing a mysterious quality or notably powerful energy, which when seen will bring you a serious message. Often these are tripled digits, such as 333, or 999, or 444. The power conveyed by these tripled numbers attempts to demonstrate that the power of that single number is effectively increased, to ask you for an even bigger and deeper look at what it is showing you.

Other numbers like 1212, or 3838, or 4114 are an example of another type of clear message that is advising you in a specific way. All of these combinations have an extreme vibration because of

The Universe Has A Number

the doubled nature of two of each number in the sequence, and have very strong and clear energy to share. All of this leads back to understanding what each number means on its own first, so as you begin to learn to interpret the magic and vibration of each number, you will be better able to explore these more fascinating and intriguing number combinations in your life.

Certain number sequences may repeat themselves frequently in your life, which is an indication that you are looking at something about your life in a manner that is insufficient with your dreams and goals, and you need to pay better attention to what is happening on your journey. Repetitive numbers are great messengers about how to help yourself move forward. Ask all of the numbers how they are wanting to communicate with you, and allow them to teach you the meaning of powerful purpose, and magic of the self and the journey of life.

Chapter 6: Birthday Numerology

The alignment of your birth number has a vibrational energy that can give you an essential understanding of your life path and purpose. It is how your energy is recommending you travel forth in this life, even as you have another career in mind, or goal, or purpose that you would prefer. Your birth vibration, or life path number, is a way for you to correlate the energy behind your essential nature or gifts with the life you are hoping to create as a unique individual.

You already learned how to calculate your birth number in the previous chapters; however, here is the basic formula for you to input your own birth information into the equation so you can find your own life path number:

Birth month + birthday + birth year

The Universe Has A Number

All of the numbers are added together until you get down to a single digit. In some instances, you may end up with a double-digit number like 11 or 22. These numbers, although a powerful life force energy, are not necessarily attributed to a life path, and have an energy of teaching a person the quality of their new path as a member of an ascended group of energies. Gandhi would be a good example of a person resonating with the numbers 11 or 22. They are called "master" numbers because of how energetically pure they are in the life force of all things. For this book, you will need to add your number all the way to the single digit for a pure life path number. So, if you end up with an 11 or a 22, go ahead and add them up like this: $11 = 1 + 1 = 2$ and $22 = 2 + 2 = 4$.

Here is another example of calculating a birth number, making sure that everything gets added until it becomes a single digit:

The Universe Has A Number

Birthdate = August 14, 1991

Month – 8

Day = 14 = 1 + 4 = 5

Year = 1991 = 1 + 9 + 9 + 1 = 20 = 2 + 0 = 2

Total Birth Number = 8 + 5 + 2 = 15 = 1 + 5 = 6

Life Path Number = 6

This is the calculation you will always use to find yours or someone else's birth number. As you read in Chapter 5, every number has an energetic quality that must be learned in order to decipher the numerical messages coming from around you. So, how does that work with your personality exactly? Each number has an essential vibration that translates into a life path concept, or quality of character, which can be shown in the following ways:

1 The Father

The Universe Has A Number

The number 1 is an energy of beginning and openness. As a number, it offers the energetic map to understanding the self through achievement and through new beginnings. People who have the life path number of 1 are shown to be the lord of life in their path to self-opening and awakening. The journey forward is known as the path of the father, not because you are an actual father, but because you sire new beginnings in every corner of your life in order to achieve your true destiny and self-purpose.

The path of the ONE is a challenge if you struggle with authority in yourself and also the authority in others. Your true path is to be your own authority and not to rely upon others to open your doors and windows for you. The last place you need to be in the life path ONE is under someone else's rule of thumb, so according to your birth number, you will need to maintain a life of authority and power as your own boss or "father," so to speak.

The Universe Has A Number

Letting yourself purposefully engage with a life that lets you do your own work and have your own say in all matters in your career is a way to honor the energy of this number. You may already have known this about yourself but haven't worked your way toward self-employment, or business ownership. The number 1 will help you get there and will always encourage you to live your life through the authority of yourself, branching out in new ways, in your own way, throughout the course for your life.

2 The Mother

The number 2 is the numerical energy of love and partnerships. The number has all of the energy of connection and heartfelt compassion and consideration for the nearest and dearest to your life, and holding onto this energy is very important for a person with the birth number of 2. The Mother is a way to describe this numerical personality vibration, because of how it lends itself to be the greatest lover of all, and who is more loving than the energy of

The Universe Has A Number

Mother? The energy of Mother does not mean that you are a mother, having given birth to a child; it means that you possess the energy of nurturing your life in a loving way in all its needs and desires.

As you mother your life, you welcome a new idea of how to bless your reality with the kind of care and nurturing required to bring you success and achievement. Every mother type has a way of letting things get out of hand though and according to this number. People born with a 2-life path need to honor their calling to be a nurturer and caregiver to their own life purpose, path, and partnerships, but need to be mindful and careful of not over-giving to other people's paths and journeys.

As a natural "mother" (even if you are a man), you may be inclined to help others with their needs and wants before contributing to your own path, not giving your own life the love that it requires. To be a balanced 2, you must be able to offer your whole life the quality of love you would give to the partnerships that are so valuable and important to you.

3 The Talented Child

The number 3 is all about creativity and working at it. You don't have to have a birth number of 3 to be a creative person; however, those born with this vibrational energy will be obviously talented at a young age in whatever gift they are born to possess, and will nurture it from the get-go. Some 3s will not be able to nurture their gift due to all of the other energies working against them, and will engage with their creative life force later in life, but as the saying should go, "Once a 3, always a 3."

If you are the "talented child," then your life will be a quest to find your talent and your tools in order to work your craft. Many artists, painters, musicians, poets, dancers, and others are 3s, but not all, of course. Some 3s are politicians who use their birth number to creatively express the laws they are hoping to pass. The point of the matter is that a 3 is born with the vibration of creative skill and builds a life around honing their craft and skill.

The power of 3 is also very strong in someone who is looking for a reason to move around the world with great frequency. Travelers of life fall under the energy of 3 and are looking for great adventures to fill their hearts with joy and creative experiences. It isn't just about what you make or do creatively; it's also about how you creatively live.

4 The Organizer

The number 4 is a large force of power, will, strength, and groundedness. This is the number of making it work and doing it in the right way, at the right time, with the right conditions. The people who are born with the birth number of 4 are very practical, pragmatic, and organized. In order to thrive, they may need a lot more financial security in order to feel happy or successful, and will want to keep all of their finances in a specific order.

The Universe Has A Number

The number 4 has a lot to do with planning ahead and preparation. People with this number are always looking for ways to reduce costs, make plans well in advance, and discourage unnecessary situations from clouding their organized lifestyle. This vibrational energy is very powerful and encourages a person with the number 4 to work within the borders of staying on top of their life tasks and work ethics.

The struggle for people born with a 4 will be that they are living a life that is disorganized, which can cause a lot of discomfort and unhappiness to their vibration. In order to feel confident in their energy, they need to live a life of comfort, stability, and organization. Most people already know this, but as you get older in your numbers (age), you learn more about how you feel best in your life, or how you like things to be a certain way. If you are a 4, knowing that you need organization in your life to feel pleasant and secure can save you a lot of discomfort down the road. So, making all of your life choices based on the knowledge of your 4 vibrations can be an incredibly useful tool to getting you grounded in your life path.

5 The Free-Spirit

The number 5 is a number that speaks of vibrational awakening in the physical body. The physical body has a lot of opportunities to evolve, grow, and transform during our lives. Those with a number 5 at the time of their birth have large, robust energy for the life of an adventurer through their contact, physical experiences, and overall health.

Most people with this vibration have a lot of interest in physical fitness, sports, diet, various kinds of health and healing in the body, and a majority of them are very aware of how things *feel*. The experience of the number 5 person is that of finding meaning, purpose, and truth in how all of their lives' moments relate to the way it makes them feel on a physical and spiritual level.

Number 5s all have potential to struggle with a variety of physical health issues, such as weight gain, poor diet, lack of exercise, and sedentary life that has no vibrancy or activity. To the 5, this can cause a life of sorrow and advises them to maintain a healthy quality of life in order to thrive. In order to feel like a happy and successful 5, putting a lot of energy into the energy of being a 5, with fitness, health, and adventuring, a 5 must focus a great deal on how they feel in their bodies.

6 The Caregiver

The 6 is a number of love in another way compared to the 2 and has a lot to do to give in the other direction. A 6 wants to help others and has a lifelong desire to extend their purpose toward giving care to the world of energy in some form or another. Not all 6s will choose this type of energy as a career, but many will foster caregiving through their personal life relationships and have a lot of times and experiences, in which they must remember to help themselves before they help others.

The Universe Has A Number

It is a problem of the 6 to overextend their own energy for the benefit of another, and this will cause imbalance in the whole life of a 6. They need to learn in their lifetimes how to give to others while they also give to themselves. The word martyr comes to mind when you come across an imbalanced 6, and many people neglect their own, real, personal energetic needs when they practice the life of a 6.

The overall love of a 6 is so strong that they are innately structured to help anyone around them, and sometimes, the best thing for a 6 to do to live a balanced life is to work in a career field that allows them to operate on all levels as a caregiver. Many of those fields help improve people's lives as we all need some kind of care at some point, and it is the work of the 6 to offer it to us all.

The Universe Has A Number

7 The Philosopher

The number 7 has a lot to do with the grace of living a life of wanting *to know*. As 7 lives their life, they spend the majority of their time questioning and seeking the knowledge to answer all of their important life questions. All of the whos, whats, wheres, whens, whys, and hows are the energy of the 7, and they need to seek as well as find the truth to all of humankind and the Universe.

Many 7s look at the world in a way that the other numbers cannot easily do, because of their inherent energy of looking for the right answers to the bigger and more important questions, while many others are content to look at only the smaller picture. To maintain your pleasure in life as a 7, you will have to look deeply into all matters that you feel connected to or interested in. The life of a 7 is one of study and contemplation and has the vibration of not just learning, but also of knowing.

The Universe Has A Number

The past, present, and future are all matters of interest to the 7, as they will always need to know the answers to where we've been, where we are, and where we are going. It is also important for a 7 birth number to engage with activities that stimulate the mind in all areas, so that the energy of life is in alignment with the vibration of the birth number. Studying in college and continuing education throughout life feels good for a 7 and keeps them in high vibration with their number.

8 The Professional

The number 8 is a number of financial success, but also of personal life success. It has the story of one who succeeds in their art, craft, or skill through the endless cycle of deliberate work required to walk the path they truly want to know. No matter who you are, you may have this idea or intention in your path, to become "the professional," but it is the 8 who has an inherent need to walk this path in order to feel in alignment with their whole truth.

8s are brave when it comes to accepting the path they must walk, for they recognize that it will be a compliment to their whole experience as a person to follow the journey of making their career an important a factor to all other parts of their lives, working together in one, infinite cycle of truth and trust.

The engineer is a good example of an 8. They continuously strive to improve and better already existing and working things in this world, in order to improve all of the energy around us, not just in their own lives. The engineer is excited to play with what they can discover, and will always tinker at the work at hand in order to find the best solution. This is a good metaphor for the birth energy of an 8. You don't need to be an engineer to express these qualities as an 8, and will want to find the path that allows you to continuously tinker with all of the work you do in this life for the benefit of your own energy.

9 The Humanitarian

The Universe Has A Number

The number 9 is a number of interests in all of the other beings in this world. It is the number of the collective consciousness of all we are and all we do, and as a 9, you will be someone who has an inherent interest in the good of all humankind, and will want to work in ways throughout your life that speaks to the ALL and not just the one. The birth path of the 9 is to elaborate on all of the known ideas from all of the numbers that come before it, in order to put us all into the perspective of equality with all other parts of the world and each other. The 9 represents unity in all numbers and is in need of a life that supports this commonality in beings.

As a 9, humanitarian work is at its most appealing for you because it encompasses all of these things, but you need not work in the field of this nature. Not everyone needs to be Mother Teresa or the Dali Lama in order to exist as a 9. You can bring that quality of energy into your life and whatever work you do in this world. The 9 will feel the most content when they are expressing their energy as a humanitarian thinker and doer, and will have a positive public influence on their lives and those around them.

As a 9, it is important to remember that the path of having this mentality or state of being can be long and difficult, as you will have many challenging life lessons to show you the true meaning of all life and knowing how all people are one life together, no matter what your birth number is. 9 birth people are the truth tellers and they bring with their vibration of energy knowledge of how to embrace all energies in the Universe.

Birth Numbers In a Nutshell

Your birth number is always a part of your journey through life. It has a way of showing you your life path and how to connect and align in the best way to enjoy and experience your true vibrational energy as the number you are born with. Many people will explore all of these energies throughout the course of their lifetime, and will want to decide on their own how they feel the best in their work, home, and personal life.

Having an idea of what your birth number is can be a very powerful way for you to concentrate and focus on this true aspect of your energetic vibration, so that you can be more open to the path you were born to.

In the next chapter, you will learn a great deal more about how a personality number can greatly influence your birth number, and it's all in a name.

Chapter 7: Forecast for the Day

As you begin to unlock and decode the secret language of numbers, you will likely have a desire to start making your own predictions about how things will work out for you. Everyone wants to be able to predict the future, and sometimes, numerology can help you discover more about how certain energies can have an impact on your future through the advice of each number.

Let's start with a day in life and see what it would like to attempt to predict your day using a simple formula, requiring only your birthday, the current month, and the day.

We will say that the birthdate is October 10, 1979. Here is a reminder of how you break that number down into a single digit:

The Universe Has A Number

October = 10 (month) 1 + 0 = 1

Day = 10   1 + 0 = 1

Year = 1979   1 + 9 + 7 + 9 = 26 = 2 + 6 = 8

So, now you have the month (1) the day (1) and the year (8) all broken down into a single digit. Now you add them up to each other like this:

1 + 1 + 8 + = 10 = 1 + 0= 1

Voila! Your Birth/Life Path number is a 1! The reason you utilize your birthdate to help you calculate your forecast is that on the day you are born, you are assigned your own birthday number that has a way of influencing your entire life experience. And as you age and grow along your journey, that number has a way of showing you how you are meant to learn along your road as a person.

The Universe Has A Number

The number will never change, but the days, months, and years that go back all have a different number every day, and allow you to project a different forecast for yourself by the daily, monthly, or even yearly number.

So, how does a number broken down like in the example above the influence and impact your day? In order to calculate your daily forecast, you will need your Birth/Life Path Number + Today's Date broken down into a single digit. Now add them together until they become a single digit.

Today's Date = 5/19/2019

$4 + 17 + 2019 = 5 + 1 + 7 + 2 + 0 + 1 + 9 = 27 = 2 + 7 = 9$

Add the Birth/Life path number you calculated above (1) to the today's date number you just calculated to get your daily forecast number:

The Universe Has A Number

$$1 + 9 = 10 = 1 + 0 = 1$$

One is your daily forecast number. In this case, the number 1 is alerting to you that as your day unfolds, you are being asked to have awareness about your motivations with yourself in your life surrounding activity, starting new projects, becoming more available to new ideas, going to the grocery store, and buying new items instead of the usual; taking a getaway to the beach or to the trail for a hike as a new exploration of your time. All of these ideas are about starting something new. Your day is asking you for a new beginning, and as you play around with the math, you can have a lot of fun waking up every morning and calculating the vibrational energy of the day. You can even do it the day before or a few days before, if you want to plan out an experience that will coordinate with your personal number for the date, based on your birthdate.

The Universe Has A Number

Using this equation can be very useful as you start to practice numerology. You can really expand this practice by looking at your life on a bigger scale. For example, look at a month ahead and get an overall number for the whole month, and then use your daily number to help you stay on track with your monthly vibrational number.

The next chapter will show you how to plan out and calculate your monthly forecast.

Chapter 8: Forecast for the Month

Why would you want to use numerology to make a monthly forecast? Having your monthly number calculated can have a wonderful way of alerting you to the best way to align yourself with your time and energy as you take a journey, plan for your future, budget money, apply for a new job or promotion, get your mortgage paid off, work on your health and fitness, and so much more.

The purpose of a monthly forecast number is to give you a good idea of how to prepare for your own experiences based on your own unique birthdate and the month number. As you have already learned, every number has a vibration, and therefore, every month of the year has a vibration. The month of April has a completely different energy than the month of December and it isn't just the weather.

The Universe Has A Number

Your monthly forecast is a way for you to take the vibrational energy of the month you are working through, and add it to your birthdate to make a new number out of those energies. Your birthday number shows you what you need to work with energetically in the current month. Let's use an example to show you how that can work.

Let's say your birthdate is January 26, 1950. Now, we can break it down into a birthday number:

January = 1 (month) = 1

Day = 26   2 + 6 = 8

Year = 1 + 9 + 5 + 0 = 16 = 1 + 6 = 7

So now you have the month (1) the day (8) and the year (7) all broken down into a single digit. Now, you add them up to each other like this:

The Universe Has A Number

$1 + 8 + 7 = 16 = 1 + 6 = 7$

Now, that you have the birth number, you can find out the significance of the month number and how you can interpret and forecast your month ahead. Let's take the month of June as an example.

June has the vibration of the number 6 as it is the sixth month in the year. So, here is how you would calculate your monthly vibration with your birth number:

$7 + 6 \text{ (June)} = 13 = 1 + 3 = 4$

Your monthly forecast number is 4. Your whole month will be affected by the vibration of the number 4, despite the fact, the month of June has a vibration of 6. The quality of your birth energy matched with

The Universe Has A Number

the energy of the sixth month, shows you how your energy will be influenced during the whole month.

The number 4 asks for stability and strength. You might be wanting to be frivolous and carefree, while the number 4 is telling you to plan carefully and stay grounded; stick to your plans and connect with your ability to stay focused on your task at hand.

While you are working on this overall energy in the month of June, you can now use your daily forecast to help you stay on track with your 4 vibrations. Each day will have a new number to represent a way for you to work within the challenges of maintaining stability from day to day. All of your daily forecast numbers would need to be read through the lens of a 4 vibrational theme to help you attract the right energy to put forth your best effort to stay grounded and secure.

The daily forecast and the monthly forecast allow you to have an idea of how to meditate on the quality of energy unfolding in your life. You may have to make some adjustments or sacrifices to live with the energy of your numerical forecast, but doing so may provide you with excellent growth opportunities, and prevent certain unwanted things from occurring so that you can live well with the energy of your whole life.

You can now take it a step further and use your monthly and daily forecast plans to help you with the energy forecast of an entire year! The next chapter will give you instructions for the best way to plan and use the energy of a numerical yearly forecast.

Chapter 9: Forecast for the Year

Once you have aligned with how to forecast your days and months with numerology, you can now extend it further in an even bigger way. The method of finding your yearly forecast is a lot similar to your projections from the previous chapter; however, in this case, you will take your birth number and add it to the current year using only the current year, your birth month, and the day, but not the year you were born. Let me explain in more detail:

Let's say your birthdate is July 24, 1987. You would calculate your birth number in the following way:

July = 7 (month) = 7

Day = 24 = 2 + 4 = 6

Year = 1987 = 1 + 9 + 8 + 7 = 25 = 2 + 5 = 7

The Universe Has A Number

So, now you have the month (7) the day (6) and the year (7) all broken down into a single digit. Now, you add them up to each other like this:

$7 + 6 + 7 + = 20 = 2 + 0 = 2$

The birth number for your life path is 2. Now, when you are calculating your yearly forecast, you will only use your birth month and day and rather than using your birth year, you will input the current year, like this:

July = 7 (month) = 7

Day = 24 = 2 + 4 = 6

Current Year = 2019 = 2 + 0 + 1 + 9 = 12 = 1 + 2 = 3

The Universe Has A Number

So, now you have the month (7) the day (6) and the **current** year (3) all broken down into a single digit. Now, you add them up to each other like this:

7 + 6 + 3 + = 16 = 1 + 6 = 7

Your yearly number is now 7. Your birth number, 2, is your life path number and describes the essence of your journey as a member of society and culture. It is how you will be known in your lifetime and how you will energetically live as a person, while you travel your path and purposefully live your way through all life matters.

Your yearly forecast decides how you will, as a 2, pass through a year, or rather what energies need to be in focus for you so that you can align yourself with your path in the most positive and beneficial way. All you have to do is understand the vibration of the number

The Universe Has A Number

7 to unfold the journey for yourself, and create a timeline or map assessment of what you may want to stay open to as you move forward through the year.

Qualifying your experiences through the use of a number overall is always of help and has a significant impact on how you make choices based on your inner knowledge, about how you will energetically approach your year as it unfolds.

Adding the monthly and daily forecast into the puzzle can help you align even more possibilities and potentialities, as you work more closely with the energy of the self in alignment with the energy of the day, month, and year.

Keep in mind that all life has to fluctuate, and come and go in its own right way, so strictly adhering to an idea of how things must be or should be will not have a positive effect on your experience. A forecast is a representation of possibilities and is not meant to govern your whole existence. It is a way for you to mentor yourself into a greater understanding of what

The Universe Has A Number

possibilities the Universe holds for you. As you work more closely with each number, all of your energy will align and come to the surface to help you better realize why these numbers are playing a part in your life role, and how to best utilize their energy as the year unfolds.

Chapter 10: Personality Number: Names and Numbers

All people are born into this world and given a name. You are told what your name is by your mother, or father, or both and have no input in how your name will be decided. A name is a wonderful way to show yourself as yourself to the whole world, and because it has no number associated with it, it has another kind of vibration: personality.

Names are personal and they say a lot about us, and how we are who we are. Your first name is more of how you represent your personality, and your full name is more of an expression of who you are and how you might relate to other people and the world around you. Behind closed doors, you might be more of your personality number, while out in the world at large, you may be more of your expression number.

The Universe Has A Number

In this chapter, we will focus only on the personality number, but as you learn how to decode your name into a number, you can use those concepts to explore your name further to determine your expression number using the same models of human qualities outlined in the previous chapter. Your expression number is your FIRST + MIDDLE + LAST name added up together into a single digit, but for now, we will only focus on the first name and add it up to look at personality. Once you learn how to do the personality number, you can take some time to play around with your expression number, and see how it correlates with your birth number and personality.

So, how would you determine how your name affects your number? The ability to transform your name into a number is quite simple; all you need is the alphabet and to assign numbers to each letter like this:

The Universe Has A Number

A = 1

B = 2

C = 3

D = 4

E = 5

F = 6

G = 7

H = 8

I = 9

J = 10

K = 11

L = 12

M = 13

N = 14

O = 15

The Universe Has A Number

P = 16

Q = 17

R = 18

S = 19

T = 20

U = 21

V = 22

W = 23

X = 24

Y = 25

Z = 26

Every letter has a number vibration because of how every culture uses language to communicate. All languages have their own alphabet to describe each sound, and all languages bear the same resemblance to how each number is identified numerically So, there won't be a great divide in the way an English name vibrates compared to a German or a French one.

In the personality number, you will find the same concepts of personality as was illustrated in the previous chapter. This means that even if your birth number is a 3 (The Talented Child), your Personality number could be a 1 (The Father). Looking back at all of those descriptions, you will be able to determine how having a birth number reflects your life path, while your personality number reflects how you walk the path in general.

Essentially, your personality number is what influences your ability to live in your personal truth, as your birth number asks you to do on your journey. To demonstrate this through 1-2 examples, see the name to number personality and birth equations below.

Sarah, Born: 7/25/1993

The Universe Has A Number

S + A + R + A + H = 19 + 1 + 18 + 1 + 8 = 1 + 9 + 1 + 1 + 8 + 1 + 8 = 29

2 + 9 = 11 = 1 + 1 = 2

Sarah's Personality Number = 2

7 + 25 + 1993 = 7 + 2 + 5 + 1 + 9 + 9 + 3 = 36 = 3 + 6 = 9

Sarah's Birth Number = 9

Sarah has the Personality of "The Mother" with the life path of "The Humanitarian." So, what does that all even mean? Interpreting is always the most fun when it comes to identifying your numerical vibration and here is how it works. Looking at your birth or life path number shows you how you are wanting to exist in the world overall, and in general in all parts of your life. Your personality number then demonstrates to you how you will perform in your life as yourself, walking toward that path.

So, in the example of Sarah, she will want to discover her path in the mindset of the humanitarian, doing work, or managing and maintaining her personal life with how she sees all people equally and deserving of the life of their own dreams and goals. Her best attempts at this may not be successful initially, or at all, unless she embraces her true personality as that of the mother.

This would not mean to literally become a mother, but rather to mother all of her life experiences through a nurturing and compassionate partnership with herself and her ambitions as a do-gooder. While Sarah seeks to become her truest self, she can understand how to interpret her best choice of getting to that place in life by using these two numbers to help guide her along her journey.

Bradley, Born: 9/13/1984

The Universe Has A Number

B + R + A + D + L + E + Y = 2 + 18 + 1 + 4 + 12 + 5 + 25 =

2 + 1 + 8 + 1 + 4 + 1 + 2 + 5 + 2 + 5 = 31 = 3 + 1 = 4

Bradley's Personality Number = 4

9 + 13 + 1984 = 9 + 1 + 3 + 1 + 9 + 8 + 4 = 35 = 3 + 5 = 8

Bradley's Birth Number = 8

Bradley has the personality of "The Organizer" (4) and a birth number of "The Professional" (8). Bradley wants to energetically support his life path by becoming his true energy as a professional, and working toward his life purpose in the manner of making it his entire experience in life. He is the devoted boss to his own profession and career goals in order to work with his true birth vibration, and to feel all of his energy on his path of life.

His personality works well with his life path as the professional, due to the fact that his name leads him to be an organized person, or not, depending on this particular Bradley's choices of living within his true vibration as a 4. Having the personality of the organizer will help Bradley stay on tasks with his professional goals and life achievements, and will also help him assess when he is not in alignment with his purpose or path.

The energy of the 4 and the 8 together is also very powerful because of how the 4 is a product of an 8, and the 8 breaks down into 4 when split in half. In this case, the energy of the 2 comes into play and it is interpreted to mean that, in order for Bradley to acquire his highest potential, he must also include the energetic vibration of "The Mother" attribute into his life work.

Names and Numbers Moving Ahead

The Universe Has A Number

All of us have our name and we use it our whole lives; however, some people will elect later in life to change their name in order to interpret their energy in a new way. It does matter how you want to portray your self through the numerical personality of your name, and if you decide to change your name to a new one as a reflection of who you truly feel you are, compared to the name you were given at birth, you will be shifting your whole energetic balance to better suit who you feel you truly are.

This is sometimes shown in the appearance of nicknames that people prefer to go by instead of their true, given name from their parents. All names matter and carry a lot of weight in the life of a person. If you are a parent and are toying with ideas for what to name your baby, you may want to consider the numerical vibration of that name before handing it over to your son or daughter. You may not be able to accurately predict what day they will be born, and having a name already picked out could change the whole numerical energy of the new life you bring into the world.

I am not saying you shouldn't pick the name ahead of time, only that if your daughter Sarah was born 6 days later than you thought and she has a different birth number than you predicted, it may make you want to reconsider her personality name number! Only kidding.

Names have value in the world of numbers and contain within them powerful, numerical energy that can resonate with you for your entire life. It doesn't matter how long you decide to keep your name, or if you determine that you will always want that name to be your number. The energy behind it will have an influence on your life in some manner, and it is appropriate to think about how you would want to change it all if given the right set of letters to describe yourself.

Chapter 11: Your Heart's Desire Number

The language of numbers is something we all learn at an early age. When you are in your elementary school classes, you are learning how to count, add, and subtract, and one day, multiply and divide the energies of all of the numbers around in the Universe as we know it. Now, think about how your lessons in math have contributed to the way you relate to all matters in life. You can't get very far without adding or subtracting one thing to or from something else at any given moment in a day. So, how can this relate to your heart's desire from the perspective of numerology and energetic vibration?

In the last chapter, you learned about how using the letters of your first name some together through numerical addition in order to compile your single digit personality number. You have also seen that

The Universe Has A Number

your birth date added together down to a single digit shows you your true life path energy and how you will manifest the most abundance and success in your lifetime.

Now that you have these two numbers calculated, you begin to estimate how your true desires will manifest for you over the course of your lifetime, and how you will attract the dynamic reality you are looking for through the energies of your life. As we all know, the heart has many desires and they are not always related to love. Sometimes, our desires align us more with the career we are wanting, or a life journey we need to take as a traveler across the globe. Sometimes, our desires relate to wealth and financial abundance in a way that puts us in contact with how to attain and receive monetary abundance. All of these desires are valid and a part of every soul's journey through life.

As you age, so too do your desires coming from the heart. You will only have a heart's desire for a period of time, and it will resonate with how you are working

The Universe Has A Number

through your life at the time of year you are living in at the present moment. It can be a really wonderful gift to give yourself, calculating what your true desires are at any given moment in life. Usually, these urges to understand your desires come very strongly into your consciousness, when you are looking for a new path or longing for something from the past. Here is how you can look at calculating your true heart's desire number to give you a path to follow along your journey:

Life path number + personality number + forecast number = heart's desire

This calculation, in its truest formula, has a way of alerting you to a certain powerful path you can choose to align more with your dreams and fantasies, about how you want your life to be as you move forward with your life path and personality numbers. The current year or month addition comes from the formula for forecasting the year, month, or day seen in chapters 6-8. The three work together well to give you the best understanding of how to align best with your heart's desire. Let's see an example of how that works:

JANE born on 12/30/1990

$12 + 30 + 1990 = 1 + 2 + 3 + 0 + 1 + 9 + 9 + 0$
$= 25 = 2 + 5 = 7$

Jane's Life Path Number $= 7$

$J + A + N + E = 10 + 1 + 14 + 5 = 1 + 0 + 1$
$+ 1 + 4 + 5 = 12 = 1 + 2 = 3$

Jane's Personality Number $= 3$

The Universe Has A Number

12 + 30 + 2019 (current year) $=$ 1 + 2 + 3 + 0 + 2
+ 0 + 1 + 9 $=$ 18 $=$ 1 + 8 $=$ 9

Jane's Yearly Forecast number $=$ 9

Now, you can take these numbers and calculate them in the heart's desire formula listed above:

Life Path + Forecast + Personality $=$ 7 + 3 + 9 $=$
19 $=$ 1 + 9 $=$ 10 $=$ 1 + 0 $=$ 1

Jane's Heart Desire $=$ 1

Now, let's explain how that works and give you an understanding of how to qualify your own calculations. Jane is a Personality of The Talented Child with the life path number of The Philosopher and her heart's desire during this current year is the 1: The Father.

The Universe Has A Number

You can calculate your heart's desire most effectively by choosing the right forecast number for you. You may want to add your forecast number into this equation to coordinate on a monthly basis or on a week-to-week, day-to-day level, although a longer period of time, such as a year, is a more effective way to trace your path to the life your heart is truly wanting.

So, looking at Jane's forecast for a year, her life path number and her personality, we arrive at a number 1 as her heart's desire. She has a talented child personality causing her to relate best to the life of a creative worker, collaborating with the energies of making something lasting that has a physical life and benefit to the world around her. Her personality number as a philosopher demonstrates that she is always relating to her work from the mental state of wanting to perceive the world from all angles and openings; and that she will best serve her life path by being open-minded to all of the ways her work and creative expression will manifest in her life. Her yearly

The Universe Has A Number

forecast number allows her to coordinate these two parts of her reality, and to add them together shows her heart's desire as a creative life path person, with the point of view of preparing to work through the intellect of seeing all sides of her problem. This leads to a heart's desire of wanting the energy of the 1 to push her forward in her path by alerting her to becoming a bigger force in her forward motion, taking a new opportunity or idea to create something bigger or better than ever before. This is how people become aligned with understanding the energy of how they want to progress and proceed on their life path. You can simply say that Jane is an artist who likes all methods of expressing her truest self as a philosopher, but currently wants to branch out in new ways with the life force and authority of a new beginning from the vibration of the number 1.

All of this assessment comes from the energy of the numbers, and as you begin to correlate these numbers, you will begin to assess where you are in your current path. There will plenty of desires that

The Universe Has A Number

shift and change with each passing month or year; however, the elements of your life path and personality will never change (unless you change your name), and will always give you the foundation for your heart's desire when added to a forecast number.

Other kinds of methods exist all over the internet and you can look for other ways to arrange and coordinate certain formulas. All of them give you a certain vibrational frequency from the sum of all the numbers. Every number will align you with a certain truth, and it is up to you to align with your intuition to interpret the best number for your current life path. Only you know the true reality of where you are and what you want, and your heart's desire number is a sure-fire way to get you thinking about the right path to getting where you want to be going.

Chapter 12: Compatibility Numbers

Love is always in the air, and as such, it is also in every number in some capacity. Love numbers are all about how your life path and personality number come together to form a single digit compared to your girlfriend, boyfriend, spouse, or other partner's numbers in life and personality. You have already learned how to calculate your Life Path number from your full birth date and your Personality number from your first name.

Now, all you have to do is add those two numbers together to find a compatibility match number to compare to another's. Let's choose a male/female compatibility partnership as an example:

ANGELA born 4/6/1989

The Universe Has A Number

And

TOM born 9/5/1991

A + N + G + E + L + A =

1 + 14 + 7 + 5 + 12 + 1 = 1 + 1 + 4 + 7 + 5 + 1 + 2 + 1 = 22 = 2 + 2 = 4

BORN 4 + 6 + 1 + 9 + 8 + 9 = 10 = 1 + 0 = 1

Angela's Compatibility Number = 4 + 1 = 5

T + O + M = 20 + 15 + 13 = 2 + 0 + 1 + 5 + 1 + 3 = 12 = 1 + 2 = 3

BORN 9 + 5 + 1 + 9 + 9 + 1 = 34 = 3 + 4 = 7

Tom's Compatibility Number = 3 + 7 = 10 = 1 + 0 = 1

The Universe Has A Number

Angela wants to be with a lover who has a physicality of a robust and energetic person, to compliment her desire for a love life that is adventurous, free-spirited, and fun. Angela is desirous of a mate who has the energy of freedom but who can also align with her need to balance her free-spirited love nature, with a more practical and grounded energy, like that of a 1, 4, or 9.

Tom is a 1 and he is looking for a romantic partner who aligns with his truths and patterns for accomplishment. He needs to find love that has a way of keeping him upbeat and more personal with the world around him, so that he can identify his cause in a more open-hearted way, rather than a cold or cynical way. Tom's need for a balanced relationship would align his love number of 1 with a 2, 5, or a 6. He needs someone who will like his need for authority, but who can soften his edges and bring more fun and freedom into his life.

The Universe Has A Number

This example demonstrates a unique way to show how two people might share compatibility. Angela and Tom would work together because of Angela's passion for adventure and a need to be tied to the ground at times. Tom's desire for attention to detail and finesse in life's patterns and path would be compatible with a partner like Angela, because of how she would energetically encourage a lightness of heart in all life matters, balancing each of their energetic love vibrations.

In order to determine your compatibility with another person's number, all you have to do is utilize the concepts of the life path number listed in Chapter 9. All of these archetypes are used throughout the course for determining your path, personality, and other matters simply because of their numeric vibration and the energy that each one possesses.

Once you have an idea of these archetypes, you can further understand how these numbers align well with each other in an energetic balance.

The Universe Has A Number

Some compatibility numbers are not related to love at all and have a lot more to do with other relationships in our lives. We all have a variety of opportunities to connect with others, and some of those matters arise in the workplace, throughout your life as a friend, or involving yourself with a couple of people or a group and determining larger compatibility from that. Even your own children have a compatibility number to consider.

All of these ideas will equally correlate with how you view the question. If your question is one of love compatibility, you will use your numbers to arrive at a love idea for how these numbers can be loving in energy, and how other numbers might be less romantic with others.

There are a lot of compatibilities that are different from love numbers. Let's use the workplace as an example of a compatibility number test:

GEORGE Born 7/19/1995

The Universe Has A Number

And

WILL Born 11/13/1988

$G + E + O + R + G + E =$

$7 + 5 + 15 + 18 + 7 + 5 = 7 + 5 + 1 + 5 + 1 + 8$
$+ 7 + 5 = 39 = 3 + 9 = 12 = 1 + 2 = 3$

George's Personality Number $= 3$

BORN $7 + 19 + 1995 = 7 + 1 + 9 + 1 + 9 + 9 +$
$5 = 41 = 4 + 1 = 5$

George's Life Path Number $= 5$

George's Compatibility Number $= 3 + 5 = 8$

$W + I + L + L = 23 + 9 + 12 + 12 = 2 + 3 + 9$
$+ 1 + 2 + 1 + 2 = 20 = 2 + 0 = 2$

The Universe Has A Number

Will's Personality Number = 2

BORN 11 + 13 ⎸ 1988 = 1 + 1+ 1 + 3 + 1 + 9 + 8 + 8 = 32 = 3 + 2 = 5

George's Life Path Number = 5

George's Compatibility Number = 2 + 5 = 7

George is an 8 and Will is a 7. George is The Professional, while Will is The Philosopher. So, how does this translate in terms of coworker compatibility? Let me show you…

George has no ideals about the workplace. He knows that all of his work has a continuous thread that alters from day to day, and always has a workflow that requires consistent and thoughtful energy put forth toward his ideals of good work performance and planning ahead with the rules of his energetic work at the office. Flowing forward with all of the patterns of the workforce and that's all there is to it.

Will is intrigued by altering assignments to better align and coordinate with new ideals and new methods that he thinks can possibly improve the energy of the workplace. He is open-minded to all of the options and isn't afraid to step out of the usual rules to try and admire a new way of looking at his work. He might even be an innovator because of his willingness to take a look at all sides of a problem.

George trusts the system because he knows it already works the way it is as Will attempts to alter the system to be more innovate in the workplace. George and Will are not compatible colleagues because of their different approaches to work matters. They may be essential elements and personalities to a bigger team for the dynamic balance of the greater good, but if they were partnered up on a project, they would end up at odds with each other.

The Universe Has A Number

Are you seeing the pattern here? Each number will have its quality that can be translated through the lens of whatever questions you are asking about your life. The Universal energy of each number will explain to you the outcomes and answer your queries through the dynamic energy they each possess.

Asking each time what you want to know first before you question the number vibration is how you get the clear answers you are looking for. Whether it is love, work, family, or friend compatibility, each number vibration will interpret these realities based on the concept of their unique and individual vibrations.

Chapter 13: Health Numbers

Health is something that seems odd when it comes to listening to your numerological reports; however, it can all be determined from a number you have already learned from in chapter 9: the life path number.

Your life path number is also called your birth number and is derived from adding the month + day + year you were born into the world. As you saw in that chapter, each number correlates with an archetype of personhood that shows the quality of energy that you express or need to express as your life unfolds.

The energy of that number corresponds with all of the other ways you can determine a numerical vibration in your life energy. For example, you learned in the last two chapters about how these archetypes are reflected by the number you get from certain equations to create your heart's desire and your compatibility. The same is true for determining all of your health inquiries, and it comes from the simple vibration of your life path number. You don't need a formula to understand this; however, you do need to see how your health can manifest through your life path number and why it is helpful to have that awareness.

In this chapter, we will review each archetype associated with each number vibration to give you a perspective of the health concerns or realities that can occur on your life path. All of them have a reference to a possibility and are not prescriptions or diagnoses; they are simply an energetic possibility that can happen when you are born with a certain life path number, and having an awareness of what each number works within the reality of health can help you ascertain the best way to care for yourself as you improve your knowledge of numbers.

1- The Father

The Universe Has A Number

How You Are: A 1 is a strong and powerful energy and looks for leadership opportunities wherever they go in life. A 1 wants to be in command of their experiences and needs a lot of energy to devote to their life as a personal force of nature and is not easily governed by others, wanting to lead the way in a dynamic way of their own making. There are a lot of problems that can arise, stemming for a need to be in control and having too much control can cause problems in the ones personal and professional relationships.

Where It Shows Up: With this life path number, you have a lot of direct energy pointed at your personal life goals and truth, or you don't, so there are two ways that this energy can manifest in your health. The first is that you can become excessive in your energy, and your patterns of work will cause you to feel too much consideration for your need to prove your power or your likes in this world. So, you strain yourself through a variety of acts like addictions to drugs and alcohol and other items, as well as an excessive need to please only yourself, leaving you alone often. This can be detrimental to your whole health as we all need people to help support us through our journey in life. Another way this can manifest is through a deficiency in your inherent nature as a powerful person, and if you are not honoring your need to walk the path of the 1 person, you will have a lot of ego-mind problems as a result of not doing anything with your mental strength. All of your thoughts will become cynical and bitter without the proper way to live as you are in the life path of "the father." Sometimes, this can also lead to addictions to substances or behaviors. All of this can appear also in the form of aches and pains in the body, and for ones, it is mostly in the hips and buttocks, knees and joint tissue as well as headaches in the brain, especially if you are deficient in your 1 power.

How to Care for Yourself: As a 1, you will always need to use your dynamic energy to force yourself forward through life. Standing still isn't a helpful way for you to care for your health and you need a lot of energy to live, so if you are lazy or inactive, you can be influencing your innate power as an individual. Regular exercise is a powerful tool for a 1, as well as avoiding addictive substances, and eating a balanced and clean diet. There are also ways for a 1 to treat their health through the use of certain forms of therapy such as Reiki and massage, to help them connect to relaxation while they support their powerful life energy.

2- The Mother

How You Are: As a 2, you are very insecure when people aren't giving you any affection. Your life is all about giving and receiving love from others and to others, and so as "the mother," you are looking for a balance between the two: giving and receiving. The energy of the 2 is that you put a lot of it into caring for others with a lot of hurts when they do not reciprocate your love. All of your life will be looking to create a good balance between loving yourself as well as you love others.

Where It Shows Up: The energy of the 2 manifests in physical ways in both the excessive and the deficient realities. Two much 2 energy leads to a martyr mentality as well as a passion for accusing others of not being enough for them. This has a lot to do

129

with the imbalance of loving the self, and it can also arrive in the form of tightness in the chest and back around the shoulders as well as skin irritations and issues of eyesight. When there is a deficiency of this energy, a 2 can feel less like a loving person and more of an embittered person who pushes love away. Energetically, this will live in your throat and you may want to be a chain smoker as a result of that, and will have a hard time talking about your feelings and emotional experiences. The energy of both can lead to a lot of traumatic partnerships that end in tears and require additional emotional support from others, giving off the energy of neediness. All of this can be felt in the heart, lungs, and eyes as well as soreness in the muscles and joints.

How to Care for Yourself: When a 2 is aligning with a lack or excess of their energy, they will need to find the right balance for them. A lot of the time, a self-love care plan is a good approach, as many 2s are looking for too much love from outside of themselves, and they need to be able to give enough to themselves before asking it of others in return. Getting a regular massage or acupuncture, organizing special alone time with yourself, eating loving foods like fruits and vegetables, avoiding drugs, alcohol, and cigarettes and doing light exercises, such as yoga, swimming, or tai chi can create an excellent balance for a 2 life path person.

3- The Talented Child

How You Are: You are all over the map emotionally because you have so much to express, both up and down, both light and dark, and it's a good thing. Many threes are the artistic type and need to be allowed to show off how they are feeling. In a culture that demands a certain kind of attitude about life, a 3 might find it hard to express themselves and can sometimes overly express as a way to maintain sanity or suppress and control their feelings, in order to hide their true nature and live within the status quo; a very unhealthy behavior for an expressive and creative 3.

Where It shows Up: Physically, this can show up in the abdomen, both upper and lower, of a person. The area above and below the belly button relates to the entire digestive system and also the reproductive organs. The digestive tract can be very sensitive to the emotional imbalances, which a 3 can bring into their life if they are not working well with their energies. Indigestion, irritable bowel syndrome, flatulence, and other digestive issues arise here. The reproductive organs can go one of two ways: dormant, frigid and silent, or overly erotic, sexually addicted, and excessive. There are many 3s who walk on a ledge, teetering between these two extremes, and find it hard to maintain a balance, which can lead to abuse of alcohol and sometimes drugs. 3s will feel some of these emotions stored in body fat including an excessive diet or weight extremes, and there will also be a presence of depression, anxiety, and occasionally paranoia.

How to Care for Yourself: If you are a 3, you need to promote a healthy lifestyle that can accommodate the ups and downs of being such an expressive person. You will need to develop a program or pattern for yourself that keeps you on top of these emotional highs or lows, so that you can quickly identify them and you are not letting them control your life journey as a creatively expressive person.

The Universe Has A Number

When you get more comfortable with identifying your patterns of emotion or expression, you will be able to add to your lifestyle with more normal activities that feel like a good balance for your health, such as occasional alcoholic beverages, eating decadent foods, and performing in front of others as you need to when the time is right. Acting on a level of security, rather than a level of emotional insecurity, is the health work of the 3.

4- The Organizer

How You Are: You are deeply concerned with financial matters and have a stable income. Your future is of great importance to you and although you feel a sense of "groundedness" in your 4 energy when you are not grounded, it makes you feel very upset on an emotional and physical level, whether you realize it or not. Those with the powerful energy of the 4 are not easily able to react to life's unexpected moments due to a need for organization and structure, and often feel the pangs of anxiety, worry, doubt, and fear when things are not going as they have so perfectly planned it out. When these issues arrive, the 4 will look for ways to treat their fears and doubts by asking for more energy from others as a way to balance the output. They need input to feel secure.

Where It Shows Up: When these imbalances occur for the 4, it can manifest in a great number of ways, but most specifically, in the kidneys and lower back area, the joints and joint tissues, and panic in the mind resulting in a powerful headache and an inability to get good rest, leading to bouts of insomnia. A 4 needs stability and having a regular routine is an integral component to the successful health of this number's energy. When a 4 looks outside of themselves for repair or for treatment, they can often feel internal neglect because they didn't look for the healing they needed from within. A 4 wants that assistance from the outside when they feel uncomfortable with their health and well-being, and in general, it is often good to seek medical advice; however, the 4 really wants to put their health into their organized lifestyle and keep track of it like they keep track of their mortgage payments.

How to Care for Yourself: A 4 will always want a way to get grounded and some of the best ways to do that are exercise and the right diet. Everyone is different and so the right kind of exercise and diet must be determined by the 4 that you are, accounting for personality and other numerical factors. Eating plenty of nutritious, organic fruits and vegetables, especially root vegetables, grains, and animal proteins, will help the 4 feel very healthy and connected to their earthly nature. Hikes in nature or sports activities that can occur outdoors are also very impactful for the energy of the 4. The organization is of great benefit to the health of the 4, so having a stricter schedule than some of the other numbers can help feel more secure, and stable health-wise and life-wise. To put a 4 out off of their schedule is like telling a dog they can't have their dinner anymore. It won't work for the 4 to live a healthy, balanced life without organizing it first.

5- The Free-Spirit

How You Are: A 5 wants to be alive, and nothing can stand in the way of that. Fives are less organized than 4s because all they need is the thrill and adventure of life in order to feel robust and happy. A 5 will listen to their intuition and instinct to make their life the one they want. However, in the matter of health, they can overextend themselves in a large way and end up with too many projects or too many commitments, out of a desire to do everything with everyone all of the time. They don't want to miss one moment of excitement, and as such, can experience the downside of burning the candle at both ends too often.

Where It Shows Up: The type of ailments a 5 will experience relate to being overwhelmed by life, because of a lack of balance with their extreme joy and excitement for life. All 5s want to be out in the world doing something, even if that just means running errands and going to the grocery store. A lot of 5s will work against their energy and not in favor of it, but looking at ways to only support their joie de vivre. Another way that 5s can imbalance themselves is in the opposite direction. Living a sedentary lifestyle, on a couch in front of the TV or computer screen, is just as detrimental, or even more so, than doing too much all the time. A 5 can experience adrenal fatigue, chronic exhaustion, and temperamental issues when they haven't had enough downtime or relaxation, issues with drugs and alcohol, and an excess of energy that can cause nervousness, fidgetiness, and ego problems. Suppressed 5 energy can look like excessive weight gain, depression, lack of drive and ambition for life, problems with eating disorders, spasms in the muscles from lack of exercise, and a variety of psychological issues like anxiety, insomnia, and depression.

How to Care for Yourself: A 5 needs to be mindful of how much is too much when it comes to making plans and getting things accomplished, even when it is fun and play. 5s need to support their need for rest and relaxation in between their need for robust and exciting life experiences that keep them busy and all over town. Suppressed 5s need to move their bodies more often, and exercise of some kind daily is the best way for a deficient 5 to work with their vibration. Even if it is just taking a walk for 30 minutes, or even doing some light stretching or yoga is good. However, many 5s feel the best with an aerobic workout at least 3-4 times per week. All Fives need to care for their internal organs with a clean and healthy diet, and many 5s work well with organic smoothies, fresh vegetable and fruit juices, and steamed foods with lower fat intake. A 5 might not like to hear this, but the last thing they need is sugar in their coffee, and it would be best not to drink coffee at all. A 5 doesn't really need caffeine to get going, and usually, all it does is create an excess of energy that leads to eventual adrenal fatigue.

6- The Caregiver

How You Are: As a caregiver, you are very good at the nurturing of others, and have a way of listening to the problems and ailments of others that is unlike any other number vibration. As a result of this, you are often connecting a large part of your energetic vibration to others who are in need and can be exposed to adopting their cares, worries, insecurities, and even illnesses and physical problems. A 6 is only well when they are providing the same support to themselves. Much like the 2, the 6 needs a lot of affection and self-care directed back toward themselves. A 6 will often answer to another's needs before their own, and can lose a lot of their health from doing this so often. They are providers as they accept another's pain as their own, and want to care for the injured and the sick as much as possible, as it is their nature to do.

Where It Shows Up: For the 6, health concerns arise in all of the areas of the body that relate to joints, joint capsules, connective tissues, and muscle fibers. There can also be a lot of insecurity in the thoughts and mind about whether you are good enough or have helped enough, or whether you are capable enough. This can cause its own set of physical ailments in the form of digestive problems, stamina issues, chronic fatigue, and deliberate cycles of binging all kinds of things, from food to TV, alcohol, and drugs, in order to fill the whole inside of yourself that is emptied regularly by trying so hard to heal other souls.

How to Care for Yourself: A 6 needs a strict self-care plan to keep them from overdoing it when it comes to helping others. Like the 2, or The Mother, a 6 needs to support themselves first and then give to others. Taking care of your body as a 6 requires some form of gentle exercise that is heart opening and grounding, so that you are in good energy to assist others in need. Taking yoga or a dance class can be very helpful for a 6, or even brisk walk outdoors would be energetically good. Diet is also of great importance and the six needs a lot of fiber and a good amount of fat in order to stay balanced. Hot baths or steamy showers at the end of a long day work wonders on the health of a 6, and having scheduled times throughout the day for personal care and alone time are a sure-fire way to provide true comfort for a 6 in need of health care. A 6 will also have an attitude of confidence and self-worth when they tend to their own needs and don't rely upon others to "cure" them of their ailments.

The Universe Has A Number

7- The Philosopher

How You Are: The 7 is the one who will use their mental abilities over their physical ones. They are always wishing to know and wanting to learn and discover, and as such, spend a great deal of their energy through their thoughts and mental state. 7s want to work it out, and they want to figure out the best solution, and sometimes, it is harder for them to see all that they need to in order to lead a balanced and fully productive life. With their needs to use their thoughts, they can also be very egotistical and arrogant about what they profess to know, alienating others and creating an aura of "know-it-all" energy that puts other people off. When a 7 is in their cups, as they say, they can often feel even more impressive than they actually are, and may need to exclude substances in their life in

order to promote a more light and friendly
balance of thoughts and feelings.

Where It Shows Up: Sevens are attracted to
information and rules of thought, and need a
lot of connection to people with authority of
information about any given subject. They will
talk to 4-5 different doctors about the same
ailment to offer themselves the most
knowledgeable outcome to their current
health issue. They are likely to discuss in great
detail all of their theories about how it should
be, and not what it actually is, when it comes
to a sickness or illness. The 7 can be very
prone to diseases of the mind, including
paranoia, schizophrenia, Alzheimer's, and
other neurological issues. They can also have a
lot of problems around the neck, jawline,
throat, and sinus cavities as a result of their
general energy being focused in the head.
When a 7 isn't feeling well, it is usually

The Universe Has A Number

exposed to them through the lumps in their
throat through a vocal cord blockage, and also
through their allergies, frequent head colds,
and other illnesses of the ears, nose, and
throat.

How to Care for Yourself: A 7 will do well to give
themselves plenty of physical activity to keep
the balance between thoughts and action, and
an excellent physical activity for the 7 is a
brisk walk for a few miles. Walking is good
for the knees, rather than running long
distances, and has a way of grounding the
headiness of the 7 while giving them time to
think as they move their body. 7 also need a
lot of sleep to rest their brains from all of the
action. If a 7 is too tired and they do not get
enough rest, then they will suffer the
consequences of the head colds, ear problems,
sinus infections, and mental health issues.
Tiredness is the opposing force of the 7, so

providing yourself with ample rest and sleep is the key to a healthy mind, body, and heart.

8- The Professional

How You Are: The professional is up at dawn and ready to begin the job at hand. Like the 4, they are twice as likely to need some stability in their home, work, and personal life in order to feel successful and healthy in both the body and the mind. The 8 is great at finding ways to take on more work as it happens to be their greatest motivation in life. Being a workaholic can be the downfall of the 8 and it can cause worse problems in the health of the mind as well as the health of the body. An 8 will look for every available chance to make their work life their top priority, and as such, they will lose life in other areas including love, family time, and chores.

The Universe Has A Number

Where It Shows Up: The excessive work plans
and career goals are tempting to the 8, and all
day long, they will benefit from their own
career ambitions. However, this can lead to a
variety of health problems including lack of
sleep, lack of healthy eating for lack of time to
make or find the right kind of food, lack of
personal joy and openness with others who
are important in your life, and lack of steam
for all of the more pleasurable parts of life
that are not related to work. Workaholics are a
group that needs to eat a lot of sugary foods
and crave rich things like fried foods or
unhealthy fats, and also have a need for
caffeine, alcohol, and sometimes prescription
drugs that take the edge off, or promote more
energy for more work. All of these things can
lead to a big imbalance in the health and
mental well-being of anyone, and especially
the 8. It can manifest through muscle
soreness, aches, and pains in the hips, low-

back, neck, and shoulders. Jaw tension is a problem here, as well as dark circles under the eyes. An 8 will also have a problem finding a lot of sleep in their life, and will end up choosing to either work or play when they should be resting, leading to more cycles of caffeine, sugar, alcohol, and poor diet.

How to Care for Yourself: The work and 8 requires a balance, as do all numbers, with life in general, especially relating to their work and career. 8 will lose their health in order to work more, making it harder for them to do good work for long stretches. Burn-out is what the 8 needs to avoid, and so finding the right attitude toward a professional life is how the 8 can nurture their health. Creating a schedule that benefits them as a whole instead of how it only benefits career, will help the 8 avoid any fatigue issues and meltdowns. Regular exercise helps keep an 8 in focus and will also activate their energy in their body as well as their mind. You can find out how to become more open to this energy when you practice self-discipline with your accounting of time and energy with each part of your life. As you get more responsible with your 8 energy, you will learn how to give yourself the gift of acceptance that all parts of your life need the same devotion that you give to your work, to create a better healthy life.

9- The Humanitarian

How You Are: The 9 is a person to foster the energy of all other numbers and wants others to thrive just as much as they do. They have a secret mission to perform, and it is all about helping other people align with their truth and urges to become themselves. As a 9, you would be more likely to focus your attention on the whole world and not just one person at a time, so your thoughts and ideas pertain to larger groups and their histories, and how the world collectively operates in a successful or unsuccessful way. To be a 9 means that you are willing to look at the big picture, and this can mean that you step far outside of your body to think about these matters before you come back down to earth and take action to help others transform their communities. 9s are prone to a lot of diseases due to their innate ability to collect the energies and feelings of larger groups of people. They need a lot of energetic support from their friends, family, and self in order to do their life path work. Some 9s will avoid their true nature in order to prevent this kind of work, and that can have a negative impact as well, leading to a depressed mental state, guilt, and shame for not being able to help others in as big a way as your energy wants and encourages you to do.

The Universe Has A Number

Where It Shows Up: For the 9, the health of the
physical body is affected in a variety of ways
including muscle and joint pain, or fatigue, hip
problems, including a need for replacements,
cardiovascular issues, headaches, and chronic
fatigue syndrome. Other ailments related to
the mental and emotional self and will show
up in the form of extreme egoism, unbalanced
emotions, heartache for what you cannot
change in the world, dementia, anxiety, worry,
guilt, fear, shame, and an impressive level of
intoxication and substance abuse.

How to Care for Yourself: Good health for the
nine revolves around quitting when you need
to believe in another cause: the cause of
yourself. These people \need to breathe the
energy of all people, places and things, and
need a long nap in the middle of the
afternoon, or a getaway to a relaxing place to
take their mind of the world's problems; to

focus more on living well while you can in the here and now. Many 9s are distant travelers who like to see the entire world in their lifetimes. Often, seeking out other cultures is a great way for the 9 to create balance, because they can learn what work is going to be the most important for them on their travels. Pleading with the world to change is not how the 9 will be successful, and so having the energy to balance out your work with your beliefs is an important part of the healing and health of a 9 life path individual. All numbers need some exercise, and the 9 will need to explore a variety of methods to enjoy their level of interest in all walks of life. Finding a variety of cultural foods can also bring the nine into a level of feeling healthy and whole. Acting on their need to aid the communities around them and the communities of the world is of great benefit to the health and well-being of a nine. Having

The Universe Has A Number

your ego left at the door will help you act in
accordance with the energy you are born with
under this vibrational energy.

Every number of the self has a unique pattern and
vibration. Understanding your own health needs is
important, and as you discern what number you are
and what problems can arise in your health, you will
be able to work with and develop the appropriate
treatment plan for your personal numerical vibration.
All ailments may need the aid of trained professionals,
and not all symptoms, illnesses, or problems listed
here may show up for you as well, as there were
several that were not included in each description.

Working with numerology is also about using your
knowledge of yourself and how you align with all of
your life, not just the numbers. Use your intuition to
answer the questions of your health, and allow your
life path number to give you the guidance you are
searching for.

Chapter 14: Career Numbers

Welcome to the opportunity of a lifetime! Your career is such an important part of who you actually want to be and not who you are trying to be. Numerology can point you in the right direction. All energy comes from yourself when it comes to choosing your own life path, and as you have learned about your birth number, it says a lot about the energy of who you are and what you are open to energetically in all of your life.

Your personality also has a strong power over how you manifest your life in accordance with your energy, and so, it is the result of these two numbers again that can align you with your career purpose. Only this time, you will use the energetic sum from your full name and not just your first name.

All of the archetypes have a general point of view about what jobs will work well with that energy.

The Universe Has A Number

Below is a list of some, but not all, possible careers or professions that will align with the certain archetypal energies of each number.

1- The Father

Business owner, entrepreneur, Chief Executive of anything, arm general, doctor, lawyer, manager, visionary, performance artist, musician, bandleader, campaign manager, politician, financial advisor, agent reporter, writer, journalist.

2- The Mother

Teacher, educator, artist (especially crafts), chef, physician, nurse, midwife, doula, mother of children, secretary, assistant, farmer, florist, wedding planner, family businesses, community organizer, parenting coach, life coach.

3- The Talented Child

Dancer, painter, sculptor, writer, performer, actor/actress, director of films and theater, designer, architect, blogger, photographer, florist, carpenter, yoga instructor.

4- The Organizer

Business manager, accountant, analyst, entrepreneur, engineer, agent, architect, sales representative, tax advisor, editor, event coordinator, assistant, professional organizer, CEO, CFO, payroll management, general management.

5- The Free-Spirit

Adventure seeker, world traveler, food critic, writer, artist, poet, nature photography, musician, dancer, performance artist, yoga instructor, public figure, actor/actress, entrepreneur, restaurateur, baker, chef, crafts in general.

The Universe Has A Number

6- The Caregiver

Nurse, family doctor, therapist, counselor, massage therapist, acupuncturist, Reiki healer, social worker, teacher, child care services, entertainment, hostess/waiter, bartender, emergency medical care, veterinarian, hospice worker, women's shelters, abuse recovery, advice columnist.

7- The Philosopher

Professor, educator, teacher, counselor, therapist, psychoanalyst, psychologist, visionary, writer, researcher, politician, creative writer, artist, drug and alcohol counselor, mentor.

8- The Professional

Entrepreneur, life coach, project manager, advisor, architect, designer, writer, philosopher, researcher, medical field, business owner, archivist, actor/actress, director, agent, musician, artist, restaurateur, politician, international business.

9- The Humanitarian

Civil engineer, environmentalist, health care worker, nutritionist, economic affairs, communications officer, agronomist, midwife, counselor, psychoanalyst, professional humanitarian officer, non-profit advisor.

All of these possible professions are simply a general guideline of potential careers that fit well with the energy of your life path number. You can determine the career number with the following formula:

Birth/Life Path Number + First Name + Last Name = Career Number

The Universe Has A Number

Here is a good example of how you can determine all of the number energies added together and also how you can relate them separately.

ELLEN SMITH Born 5/16/1982

$E + L + L + E + N + S + M + I + T + H =$

$5 + 12 + 12 + 5 + 14 + 19 + 13 + 9 + 20 + 8 =$

$5 + 1 + 2 + 1 + 2 + 5 + 1 + 4 + 1 + 9 + 1 + 3 + 9$
$+ 2 + 0 + 8 = 54 = 5 + 4 = 9$

Born $5 + 16 + 1982 = 5 + 1 + 6 + 1 + 9 + 8 + 2$
$= 32 = 3 + 2 = 5$

Ellen Smith's Career Number $= 9 + 5 = 14 =$
$1 + 4 = 5$

Ellen has the career path number of the Free-Spirit and the energy of the number 5 from a point of numerical energy. Her life would be best suited to something that gives her some creative freedom, and having a career or profession that will not limit her insight, intuition, and vibrant ideas will help her feel the most successful in her life. She has the life path number of the talented child, meaning that she may be mostly drawn to the creative arts as her profession and will need to have a lot of freedom to express her gift, without being restricted, advised, pinned down, or pigeon-holed. Her humanitarian 9 shows that her creative work will be best suited to helping a large organization or community, which appreciates her talents and improves as a result of her creative offerings.

As you can see from this example, you can get an overall sense of how your career will be a part of your numerical output from your life path number and your full name. If you feel compelled to use your middle name, you are welcome to incorporate it, but only if it is the name you use for your professional endeavors.

The Universe Has A Number

You can interpret the overall career number using the ideas of the name numerology with the birth date, to get a more defined and clear idea of how your career can manifest for you in your world.

Chapter 15: Numerology and Money

Numbers and money are a given. When you see a dollar amount, you see numerology. It has its energy in all of the ebb and flow of cash, receipts, transactions, investments, gambling, stock and trade, and all of the manifestations of energetic cash flow.

Many people are looking for ways to improve the energy of their money, and many use numerology as a tool to discover how to play and win and how to invest and get back a bigger numerical vibration.

Bringing into a pattern of energy that came from your birth number, first, name, forecast and career number, you can find the best way to improve your dollar amount from what it is to what you want it to be. Let's take the same example from the last chapter, using Ellen Smith's first name only, her birth date, career number, and the date she is looking to ask herself for the best numerology for any of the following financial expressions: payday, raise, investment, gambling, playing the lottery, paying off debts, and savings.

ELLEN Born 5/16/1982

Ellen's Personality Number $=$ 7

$5 + 12 + 12 + 5 + 14 = 5 + 1 + 2 + 1 + 2 + 1 + 4$
$= 16 = 1 + 6 = 7$

Ellen's Birth Number $=$ 5

Ellen's Career Number $=$ 5

Let's say Ellen wants to invest money in the stock market, and she wants to find out if certain numerological energy can support her investment. She is hoping to invest on 4/22/2019, and so that forecast number is her life path number + the date of the investment. Broken down, that formula will look like this:

Personality # + Birth # + Career # + Investment Date = yes/no/maybe

The sum of all of the numbers will be interpreted as a yes, a no, or a maybe in regard to your question of making the investment on this date. All numbers have a certain way of informing you about certain situations and can alter and shift depending on the question you are asking. An investment question that adds up to an 8 will have a different answer for you than if you asked a question about savings and loans and get the same number 8.

Let's add up Ellen's investment question to interpret her numerology for it:

The Universe Has A Number

Personality = 7

Life Path — 5

Career = 5

Investment Date = 4 + 22 + 2019 = 4 + 2 + 2
+ 2 + 0 + 1 + 9 = 20 = 2 + 0 = 2

7 + 5 + 5 + 2 = 19 = 1 + 9 = 10 = 1 + 0
= 1

The sum of this Investment query is number 1, and in terms of numerology, this is an excellent number to receive in regard to an investment. 1 is a number about authority, taking steps forward, leadership, productivity, and ownership. The number 1 is saying "yes" to Ellen's question about investment on this specific date.

The Universe Has A Number

If you want to get more advanced with your numerology predictions, you can include the dollar amount into the equation as well. However, for the purposes of understanding the simplicity of numbers, all we need in this book are the simple yes/no/maybe answers.

Here is how the numbers will break down from the point of view of the following money related projections:

- Investments
- Gambling/Poker
- Savings and Loans
- Income
- Debt

The Universe Has A Number

Number 1

Investments: Yes.

Gambling/Poker: Only if it has a way of improving the hand as in the case of the ACE, but not the dice (i.e. snake eyes).

Savings and Loans: Always a good answer for opening a saving account, but perhaps needs more thought about asking for loans.

Income: Maybe, but probably asking for an encouragement to ask for a higher income amount or a raise than what is offered.

Debt: Asks you to finance your life better to manage your debts and get organized with your overspending attitudes.

Number 2

Investments: No, because of the duality of it being a bad or a good investment and not having clarity about how it will play out after giving money away to the investment.

Gambling/Poker: No, because it is often negative in the gambling world and takes you over the amount you are looking for. In poker it can be a wise amount to add into your bets, so in case of chips and betting, yes.

Savings and Loans: Yes.

Income: Yes, for the number doubles your income or saving amount energetically.

Debt: No, because it energetically doubles on your debt, or overspending attitudes.

Number 3

Investments: Absolutely! 3 is a powerful number in the investment world and have a strong vibration of tripling on your return investments.

The Universe Has A Number

Gambling/Poker: Definitely, yes. 3 is a powerful number for a poker player and has a lot of added benefit in the rolling of dice when you roll 6s and 9s, which are products of the number 3.

Savings and Loans: Answering this question assesses what kind of savings amount you NEED or the loan amount you NEED. You may be only asking for a lower amount from a loan officer, or think you need to set aside a smaller amount for something, and 3 wants you to triple your savings and loans for your needs.

Income: Always. Answers like this always mean that it is saying yes to your question of should I, or how much is it.

Debt: No. As a result of debts tripling, you are on your way to bankruptcy.

Number 4

The Universe Has A Number

Investments: Not yet. The number four asks you to wait for another date or time to invest as it has official energy of making sure you remain stable and cautious.

Gambling/Poker: Always.

Savings and Loans: Always.

Income: No, because it is saying that your income needs more grounding and stability than you currently have. It may be offering you the answer to your question about whether you should take a job offer based on the dollar amount, or whether it is a good enough raise for you as a professional.

Debt: Yes. Number 4 in regard to debt, answers the question of how to get out of debt. Careful planning, organization, and prudence are the art of 4 in regard to debt in your life.

Number 5

The Universe Has A Number

Investments: Only if you are already financially secure.

Gambling/Poker: Always.

Savings and Loans: Not yet, wait a little longer to dip into your saving account or ask for a loan.

Income: Always.

Debt: Never, because it equates with frivolous, free-spirited spending.

Number 6

Investments: Only when you have a leftover sum that you can reinvest and you are putting an already existing sum from another investment back into the pool of available return.

Gambling/Poker: Always.

Savings and Loans: Always. Affordability comes from the energy of making a living loving yourself in the assessment of your money. 6 is all about taking care of your future in a long-term way, and provides the energy of quality of life coming from proper savings and quality loans.

Income: No. forward motion along your career income needs other numbers to feel fully successful (see other numbers on 'income').

Debt: Always, because debts need your attention and care to remove them from your life and to improve your financial well-being.

Number 7

Investments: Yes. Yes. Yes.

Gambling/Poker: Always.

Savings and Loans: Never, because it is an arrangement through another institution and puts your bank in charge of your dollars.

Income: Always.

The Universe Has A Number

Debt: Never, because you need to profit from your life and afford it without going into debt through whimsical spending and lack of accounting.

Number 8

Investments: Always and never at the same time. Confused? The 8 has a lot to do with the lifestyle of money, and how it organizes itself energetically is that it vibrates only with what is of benefit to you at the right moment and never in the wrong one. So; it's a risk either way that you have to take, or not take.

Gambling/Poker: Never. Important note: an 8 can be lucky in specific gambling and poker situations and have to be addressed at the right moment within the right game you are playing at the time.

Savings and Loans: Ask and you shall receive. The number 8 asks you to ask for the right dollar amount for your loan and the right amount of savings to save for your specific purposes. All you have to do is trust your instinct on this one.

Income: No, because it is showing you that you haven't asked for the right dollar amount for yourself and that you won't improve your income until you do.

Debt: Always, because it helps you to work with what you've got so you can pull yourself out of debt, rather than working with what you don't have to pretend like you have more money than you actually do.

Number 9

Investments: Problems arise with this investment number, showing that your investment will look stable at first, but will then turn in an unfortunate or problematic direction suggesting a different date, or dollar amount, or purpose to invest in at the time of your question.

Gambling/Poker: Always.

The Universe Has A Number

Savings and Loans: Ask for what you truly want from your accountant at this time. Ask how it will help you to have a larger or lesser number for a saving account or a loan. Working with an accountant to help you secure the right dollar amount will be useful with this vibration, so that you can achieve the perfect level of financial energy for these purposes.

Income: Always, and ask for all of the money you think you deserve and then some more on top of that.

Debt: Always.

Zero

Questions that come up will never answer you with a zero when you are calculating the numerology of dollars and cents; however, the zero is a way for you to advance your understanding of how to calculate your worthwhile you are seeking answers. When you are asking a question about your money and you are gambling with 500 dollars, but you ask if you should bet 5,000, the energy of the question will let you know what will work the best when it comes to the zero.

The energy of numbers is huge when it comes to the dollar amount, and using numerology in conjunction with your financial situation and advancement is honestly fun and enjoyable. You can take your predictions to the market and work out the numbers as you assign investments and try to understand the energy of numbers through financial predictions; you can use numerology to place your bets in poker and win a hand at the table; you can use numerology to allow your debts to become less and even paid off, by choosing the right spending path; and you can calculate savings, loans, and the best opportunity to advance your income by asking the numbers for advice.

However you apply it, numbers will always talk back, especially with your dollars and cents, so practice, play, and win!

The Universe Has A Number

Conclusion

Every person has a number, and all you have to do to find your magic number is to follow the answers of the Universe, guiding you along the way, like breadcrumbs on the trail of life. All of us are looking for a way to discover deeper meaning in the way the Universe works and teaches us its language. What you find through numerology is the lesson of a lifetime, and with each number you get to know better, the more energy you will draw upon to find the real frequency of yourself, your soul, and your life.

Plan on a lot of excitement as you unravel the secret truths around the house, at your workplace, with your own family, and all of the realms of possibility that you encounter in daily life. Bring the language and knowledge of numbers with you everywhere you go, and fall into the magic of looking beyond what is right in front of you.

The Universe Has A Number

All of the secrets of the Universe can be seen through a gateway of living with numerology, and your basic understanding from this beginner's guide is enough to get you started with the life you are asking for through the secrets of numbers. Ask and you shall receive as the numbers will be your guide and instructor on your path to influencing your life through numerology.

Moving forward, look at all of the ways a number impacts your life already. Find the places that exist in your common reality that is always tied to a specific number. Learn from it and teach yourself how all of these numbers reflect your current lifestyle, profession, romantic partnerships, health, success and more.

Give yourself the gift of knowledge by studying the secrets of numerology, and let each number or sequence of numbers show you the way!

The Universe Has A Number

Donald B. Grey

The Universe Has A Number

Connect with us on our Facebook page

www.facebook.com/bluesourceandfriends and stay

tuned to our latest book promotions and free

giveaways.